101+

HURRY-UP

HAMBURGER

RECIPES

D1120138

PUBLICATIONS INTERNATIONAL, LTD.

Louis Weber, C.E.O.
Publications International, Ltd.
7373 North Cicero Avenue
Lincolnwood, Illinois 60646

Permission is never granted for commercial purposes.

Manufactured in Yugoslavia.

ISBN: 1-56173-068-8

Library of Congress Catalog Card Number: 90-63302

Photography on pages 18 and 24 by Winston Studios Inc., Tucson.

Remaining photography by Sacco Productions Limited/Chicago.
Photographers: Catherine Money
Laurie Profitt
Styling/Production: Betty Karslake
Paula Walters
Food Stylists: Janice Bell
Donna Coates
Becky Roller (front cover)

Pictured on front cover (*clockwise from top right*): Tacos Suave de Carne con Salsa Roja *(page 35)*, Wild Rice Soup *(page 7)*, Thai Beef Salad with Cucumber Dressing *(page 54)*.

Pictured on back cover *(clockwise from top right)*: Burgers Pacific *(page 40)*, Quick and Easy Tamale Pie *(page 70)*, Wonton Soup *(page 12)* and Beef with Snow Peas & Baby Corn *(page 58)*.

Microwave ovens vary in wattage and power output; cooking times given with microwave directions in this book may need to be adjusted.

101+
HURRY-UP
HAMBURGER
RECIPES

There's no better way to start off a party or satisfy a between-meal craving than with one or more of these delectable appetizers. Since protein-packed hamburger is the key ingredient in each fabulous recipe, you will find these selections as good for you as they are delicious!

Mini Meat Pies

½ pound lean ground beef,
    browned and drained
2 hard-cooked eggs, finely
    chopped
¼ cup BORDEN® or MEADOW
    GOLD® Sour Cream
1 tablespoon chopped parsley
1 teaspoon WYLER'S® or STEERO®
    Beef-Flavor Instant Bouillon
1 (11-ounce) package pie
    crust mix

Preheat oven to 400°F. In medium bowl, combine all ingredients except pie crust mix; mix well. Prepare pie crust mix as package directs. Divide dough in half. On floured surface, roll out half the dough to 10×13-inch rectangle, ⅛ inch thick; cut into 20 (2½-inch) squares. Spoon 1 heaping teaspoon meat mixture in center of each square; fold as desired. Repeat with remaining dough and meat mixture. Place 1 inch apart on ungreased baking sheets. Bake 12 to 15 minutes or until lightly browned. Serve hot. Refrigerate leftovers.

Makes about 40 appetizers

Crispy Wontons

½ pound lean ground beef
½ pound ground pork
½ cup minced green onions
1 tablespoon cornstarch
2 tablespoons soy sauce
1 package (1 ounce) HIDDEN
    VALLEY RANCH® Milk Recipe
    Original Ranch® salad
    dressing mix
6 dozen wonton skins
2 egg whites, beaten
    Vegetable oil, for deep frying
2 cups prepared HIDDEN VALLEY
    RANCH® Original Ranch®
    salad dressing

In large bowl, combine beef, pork, onions, cornstarch, soy sauce and dry salad dressing mix; stir well. Place a small mound of mixture in center of each wonton skin. With your fingers, rub a bit of egg white on two top edges of wonton skin. Press skin together in half to form triangle, making sure skin is sealed on all sides. Place two long points of triangle on top of each other and seal with egg white.

In deep fryer or deep saucepan, heat ½ inch oil to 375°F. Fry wontons, a few at a time, until golden. Remove with slotted spoon and drain on paper towels. Serve warm with prepared salad dressing for dipping.

Makes 6 dozen wontons

Mini Meat Pies

Wild Rice Soup

½ cup uncooked wild rice
1 pound lean ground beef
1 can (14½ ounces) chicken broth
1 can (10¾ ounces) condensed cream of mushroom soup
2 cups milk
1 cup shredded Cheddar cheese
⅓ cup shredded carrot
1 package (.4 ounce) HIDDEN VALLEY RANCH® Buttermilk Recipe Original Ranch® salad dressing mix
Chopped green onions with tops

Cook rice according to package directions to make about 1½ cups cooked rice. In Dutch oven or large saucepan, brown beef; drain off excess fat. Stir in rice, chicken broth, cream of mushroom soup, milk, cheese, carrot and dry salad dressing mix. Heat to a simmer over low heat, stirring occasionally, about 15 minutes. Serve in warmed soup bowls; top with green onions. Garnish with additional green onions, if desired.   *Serves 6 to 8*

Mini Beef Tostadas

1 pound ground beef
1 tablespoon instant minced onion
1 can (8 ounces) refried beans
1 can (4 ounces) chopped green chilies, if desired
½ cup bottled taco sauce
4 dozen round tortilla chips
1 cup (4 ounces) shredded Cheddar cheese

1. Cook and stir beef and onion in large skillet over medium heat until beef is no longer pink, about 10 minutes; drain and discard drippings.

2. Stir in beans, chilies and taco sauce; cook and stir until bubbly, about 4 minutes. Spoon about 1 heaping tablespoon of the beef mixture on top of each tortilla chip; sprinkle with cheese. Place on baking sheets.

3. Bake in preheated 375°F oven until cheese is melted, about 2 minutes.   *Makes 4 dozen*

Beefy Broccoli & Cheese Soup

2 cups chicken broth
1 package (10 ounces) frozen chopped broccoli, thawed
¼ cup chopped onion
¼ lb. ground beef
1 cup milk
2 tablespoons all-purpose flour
4 ounces sharp Cheddar cheese, shredded
1½ teaspoons chopped fresh oregano or ½ teaspoon dried leaf oregano
Salt and freshly ground pepper
Hot pepper sauce

Bring broth to boil in medium saucepan. Add broccoli and onions; cook 5 minutes or until broccoli is tender.

Meanwhile, brown ground beef in small skillet; drain. Gradually add milk to flour, mixing until well blended. Add with ground beef to broth; cook, stirring constantly, until mixture is thickened and bubbly.

Add cheese and oregano; stir until cheese is melted. Season with salt, pepper and hot pepper sauce to taste.   *Makes 4 to 5 servings*

Beefy Stuffed Mushrooms

1 pound lean ground beef
2 teaspoons prepared horseradish
1 teaspoon chopped chives
1 clove garlic, minced
¼ teaspoon pepper
18 large mushrooms
⅔ cup dry white wine

1. Thoroughly mix ground beef, horseradish, chives, garlic and pepper in medium bowl.

2. Remove stems from mushrooms; stuff mushroom caps with beef mixture.

3. Place stuffed mushrooms in shallow baking dish; pour wine over mushrooms. Bake in preheated 350°F oven until meat is browned, about 20 minutes.

Makes 1½ dozen

Wild Rice Soup

Festive Cocktail Meatballs

1½ pounds ground beef
1 cup MINUTE Rice
1 can (8 oz.) crushed pineapple in juice
½ cup finely shredded carrot
⅓ cup chopped onion
1 egg, slightly beaten
1 teaspoon ground ginger
1 bottle (8 oz.) prepared French dressing
2 tablespoons soy sauce

Mix ground beef, rice, pineapple, carrot, onion, egg and ginger in medium bowl. Form into 1-inch meatballs. Place on greased baking sheets. Bake at 400°F for 15 minutes or until browned.

Meanwhile, mix together dressing and soy sauce. Serve meatballs with dressing mixture.

Makes 50 to 60 meatballs

Cheesy Beef Puffs

½ lb. lean ground beef
1 garlic clove, minced
1 egg, beaten
1 teaspoon prepared horseradish
1½ teaspoons chopped fresh thyme or ½ teaspoon dried leaf thyme
¼ teaspoon salt
Freshly ground pepper
1 package (17¼ ounces) frozen puff pastry, thawed
1 cup (4 ounces) shredded Cheddar cheese

Preheat oven to 375°F.

Brown ground beef in medium skillet. Drain. Add garlic; cook until tender. Combine egg, horseradish, thyme, salt and pepper in medium bowl. Add ground beef mixture; mix lightly.

Roll one pastry sheet to 13×10-inch rectangle; cut in half lengthwise. Spread ¼ of meat mixture over each half; sprinkle each half with ¼ cup cheese. Roll, jelly roll style, from one long side; cut into 1-inch pieces. Place, seam side down, on greased cookie sheet. Repeat with remaining pastry and filling.

Bake 15 minutes or until puffed and golden brown.

Makes about 4 dozen

Mexi-Beef Bites

1 pound ground beef
1 cup (4 ounces) shredded Cheddar cheese
1 cup (4 ounces) shredded Monterey Jack cheese
1 can (4 ounces) chopped green chilies, drained
½ cup bottled green taco or enchilada sauce
2 large eggs, beaten
Tortilla chips (optional)

Cook and stir beef in large skillet over medium-high heat until beef loses pink color. Pour off drippings. Stir in cheeses, chilies, taco sauce and eggs. Transfer mixture to 8×8-inch baking pan. Bake at 350°F 35 to 40 minutes or until knife inserted in center comes out clean and top is golden brown. Cool in pan 15 minutes. Cut into 36 squares. Serve with tortilla chips.

Makes 36 appetizers

Recipe courtesy of **National Live Stock & Meat Board**

Creamy Olive French Delight

¼ lb. lean ground beef
1 (8-ounce) package cream cheese, softened
3 tablespoons chopped green olives with pimientos
2 tablespoons green onion slices
Salt and freshly ground pepper
1 French bread loaf

Brown ground beef in small skillet. Drain. Cool slightly.

Combine cream cheese, olives and onions in medium bowl, mixing until well blended. Add ground beef; mix lightly. Season with salt and pepper to taste.

Cut ends off bread loaf; discard or reserve for another use. Cut loaf into 5-inch pieces. Remove centers, leaving hollow ¼-inch shell; discard or reserve centers for another use. Stuff bread with ground beef mixture; wrap securely. Chill until firm. Cut into slices.

Makes approximately 1½ dozen

Festive Cocktail Meatballs

Tijuana Taco Dip

1 can (16 ounces) refried beans
1 can (8 ounces) tomato sauce, divided
1¼ teaspoons TABASCO® pepper sauce, divided
1 large tomato, chopped
¾ cup shredded Monterey Jack cheese
¾ pound ground beef
2 teaspoons chili powder
1 cup sliced ripe olives
1 cup shredded Cheddar cheese
1 cup sour cream
  Chopped green onions, chopped tomatoes, ripe olive slices and cilantro for garnish
  Taco or tortilla chips

Preheat oven to 350°F. In medium bowl combine refried beans, 3 tablespoons tomato sauce and ½ teaspoon TABASCO® sauce; mix well. Spread evenly in 1½-quart baking dish. Top with chopped tomato and Monterey Jack cheese.

In large skillet cook beef and chili powder; stir frequently until meat is cooked. Remove from heat; drain off fat. Stir in remaining tomato sauce, sliced olives and remaining ¾ teaspoon TABASCO® sauce. Spread evenly over cheese. Sprinkle with Cheddar cheese.

Bake 15 to 20 minutes or until cheeses melt and beans are hot. Remove from oven. Top with sour cream. Garnish with green onions, tomatoes, olives and cilantro. Serve warm with taco or tortilla chips.

Makes 12 appetizer servings

Beef and Lettuce Bundles

1 pound ground beef
½ cup green onion slices
1 medium garlic clove, minced
⅔ cup chopped water chestnuts
½ cup chopped red pepper
1 tablespoon soy sauce
1 tablespoon seasoned rice vinegar
2 tablespoons chopped cilantro
1 or 2 heads leaf lettuce, separated in leaves and outer leaves discarded
  Hoisin sauce (optional)

Brown ground beef in medium skillet. Drain. Add onion and garlic. Cook until tender. Stir in water chestnuts, red pepper, soy sauce and vinegar. Cook, stirring occasionally, until red pepper is crisp-tender and most of liquid evaporates.

Stir in cilantro. Spoon ground beef mixture onto lettuce leaves; sprinkle with hoisin sauce, if desired. Wrap lettuce leaf around ground beef mixture to make appetizer bundle.

Makes 8 appetizer servings

Beefy Nachos

1 pound ground beef
¼ cup chopped onion
⅓ cup A.1.® Steak Sauce
5 cups tortilla chips
1 cup shredded Monterey Jack cheese (4 ounces)
  Dairy sour cream, optional
1 cup chopped tomato, optional
¼ cup ORTEGA® Diced Green Chiles, optional
¼ cup sliced pitted ripe olives, optional

In large skillet, over medium-high heat, brown beef and onion; drain. Stir in steak sauce. Arrange tortilla chips on large heatproof platter. Spoon beef mixture over chips; sprinkle with cheese. Broil, 6 inches from heat source, for 3 to 5 minutes or until cheese melts. Top with sour cream, tomato, chiles and olives if desired. Serve immediately.

Microwave: In 2-quart microwave-safe bowl, combine beef and onion; cover. Microwave at HIGH (100% power) for 5 to 6 minutes or until browned; drain. Stir in steak sauce. In 9-inch microwave-safe pie plate, layer half of each of the chips, beef mixture and cheese. Microwave at HIGH for 2 to 3 minutes or until heated through. Top with half of desired toppings. Repeat with remaining ingredients.

Makes 6 servings

Tijuana Taco Dip

Wonton Soup

2 green onions
¼ lb. extra-lean ground beef
¼ cup finely chopped celery
1 tablespoon finely chopped
   fresh parsley
¼ teaspoon salt
   Dash of pepper
12 to 18 wonton skins
6 cups chicken broth
½ cup spinach or bok choy
   leaves, halved lengthwise,
   shredded
¼ cup shredded carrot

Reserve one green onion top for garnish; chop remaining green onions. Combine chopped green onions, ground beef, celery, parsley, salt and pepper in small bowl; mix lightly.

Place approximately 1½ tablespoonfuls ground beef mixture in center of each wonton square. Lightly dampen edges of square with water. Bring together corners; pinch to seal. Set aside.

Bring broth to boil in large saucepan; reduce heat to medium. Add ½ of wontons; simmer 4 minutes. Remove cooked wontons with slotted spoon; keep warm. Repeat with remaining wontons.

Cut reserved green onion top into thin diagonal slices. Add to hot broth with spinach and carrot. Place wontons in soup bowls. Top with broth mixture.   *Makes 6 servings*

Beef and Pistachio Pâté

6 ounces sliced beef bacon
½ cup finely chopped onion
3 cloves garlic, minced
2 tablespoons butter or margarine
2 pounds lean ground beef
½ cup fresh bread crumbs
⅓ cup shelled pistachio nuts
¼ cup snipped parsley
2 tablespoons brandy
1 egg, beaten
1½ teaspoons salt
¾ teaspoon dried thyme, crushed
½ teaspoon pepper
⅛ teaspoon ground nutmeg

Line bottom and sides of 9×5-inch pan with bacon; reserve 4 slices. Cook and stir onion and garlic in butter in medium skillet over medium-high heat 3 minutes; cool. Combine ground beef, onion mixture, bread crumbs, nuts, parsley, brandy, egg, salt, thyme, pepper and nutmeg in large bowl; mix lightly but thoroughly. Press mixture firmly into bacon-lined pan; cover with reserved bacon. Set pan in 11¾×7½-inch baking dish on lowest rack of oven. Pour 1 quart boiling water into dish. Bake at 350°F 1½ hours. Remove pan from water. Fit another pan directly on top of pâté; add 3 pounds of weight (canned goods) and let rest 3 hours in cool place. Refrigerate, covered, 24 hours. Remove top bacon; invert and slice.
   Makes 8 to 10 appetizer servings

Recipe courtesy of **National Live Stock & Meat Board**

Goat Cheese Tarts

6 ounces lean ground beef
1 large onion, chopped
¼ cup chopped mushrooms
¼ cup sun-dried tomatoes, finely
   chopped
2 tablespoons sour cream
1 tablespoon chopped fresh basil
   or 1 teaspoon dried leaf basil
½ teaspoon Worcestershire sauce
   Pastry for single-crust 9-inch pie
4 ounces goat cheese or feta
   cheese
   Pitted ripe olives, halved or
   quartered

Preheat oven to 425°F.

Brown ground beef in medium skillet. Drain. Add onions and mushrooms; cook until tender. Stir in tomatoes, sour cream, basil and Worcestershire sauce; set aside.

Roll out pastry to ⅛-inch thickness. Cut into 2-inch rounds. Press rounds into mini muffin cups. Fill with ground beef mixture; top with cheese and olives.

Bake 10 minutes or until pastry is golden brown.
   Makes about 30 appetizers

Wonton Soup

Nutty Cheese-Beef Crudites

Preparation time: 10 minutes

½ pound ground beef
¼ cup chopped walnuts
3 ounces Neufchatel cheese, softened
3 tablespoons finely chopped green onions with tops
¼ teaspoon salt
Dash of pepper
24 vegetable pieces (zucchini, cucumber or jicama slices; red, green or yellow bell pepper, cut into 1½ inch squares; or pea pods, blanched and split)
1 tablespoon sliced green onions with tops

Place walnuts in 1-cup microwave-safe glass measure. Microwave at High 4 to 5 minutes or until lightly browned, stirring after 2 minutes. Break up ground beef with a fork; place in microwave-safe sieve or colander. Place sieve in microwave-safe bowl. Microwave at High 2½ minutes. Pour off drippings and place beef in same bowl. Stir in Neufchatel cheese, chopped green onions, walnuts, salt and pepper. Microwave at High 2 to 2½ minutes. Top or fill desired vegetable pieces with one rounded teaspoon of meat mixture. Garnish each appetizer with sliced green onion.

Microwave cooking time: 8½ to 10 minutes   *24 appetizers*

Recipe courtesy of **National Live Stock & Meat Board**

Eggplant Appetizer

1 medium eggplant (about 1 pound)
¼ lb. lean ground beef
¼ cup finely chopped onion
1 large garlic clove, minced
1 large tomato, chopped
1 small green bell pepper, finely chopped
¼ cup diced green olives
2 tablespoons olive oil
1 teaspoon white wine vinegar
1 tablespoon chopped fresh oregano or 1 teaspoon dried leaf oregano
Salt and freshly ground black pepper

Preheat oven to 350°F.

Pierce eggplant with fork; place in shallow baking pan.

Bake 1 hour or until skin is wrinkled and eggplant is soft. Set aside until cool enough to handle.

Meanwhile, brown ground beef in medium skillet. Drain. Add onion and garlic; cook until tender.

Peel eggplant; cut into small cubes. Combine eggplant, ground beef mixture, tomatoes, green peppers and olives in medium bowl. Whisk together oil, vinegar and oregano in small bowl. Add to eggplant mixture; mix lightly. Season with salt and pepper to taste.

Serve with toasted pita wedges as an appetizer or serve on lettuce leaves as a first course.

Makes about 8 servings

Meatballs in Spicy Red Pepper Sauce

Preparation time: 45 minutes
Cooking time: 12 to 15 minutes

1 pound ground beef
1 red bell pepper
3 tablespoons dry bread crumbs
1 egg, beaten
2 tablespoons chopped parsley
2 cloves garlic, minced
¾ teaspoon salt
¼ teaspoon ground red pepper
1 tablespoon olive oil
1 small onion, finely chopped
2 cloves garlic, minced
½ cup ready-to-serve beef broth
1 teaspoon cornstarch
½ cup dry white wine
1 tablespoon tomato paste
½ teaspoon dried thyme leaves

Place red bell pepper on rack in broiler pan so surface of pepper is 3 to 5 inches from heat source. Broil 10 to 15 minutes or until skin blisters, turning occasionally. Place pepper in paper bag; close and let stand 15 to 20 minutes to loosen skin. Meanwhile, combine ground beef, bread crumbs, egg, parsley, garlic, salt and ground red pepper, mixing lightly but thoroughly. Shape meat mixture into 35 meatballs, using about 1 teaspoon for each. Place on rack in open roasting pan; reserve. Remove loosened skin and seeds from pepper; cut into ¼-inch pieces. Heat oil in large skillet over medium-high heat. Add onion and garlic; cook and stir 2 to 3 minutes. Combine broth and cornstarch. Add broth mixture, wine, tomato paste, thyme and red pepper pieces to pan. Cook over low heat 10 to 12 minutes or until slightly thickened, stirring occasionally. Meanwhile, bake meatballs in 325°F oven 10 minutes. Remove meatballs; drain on paper towels. Stir meatballs into sauce; serve hot. *Makes 4 servings*

Recipe courtesy of **National Live Stock & Meat Board**

Beef & Corn Gumbo

½ lb. ground beef
¾ lb. fresh okra or 1 (10-ounce) package frozen okra, thawed
1 small onion, chopped
1 garlic clove, minced
5 cups chicken broth
4 medium tomatoes, chopped
1 cup whole-kernel corn, fresh or frozen
3 parsley sprigs
1 bay leaf
1½ teaspoons chopped fresh thyme or ½ teaspoon dried leaf thyme
⅛ teaspoon ground red pepper (optional)
Salt and freshly ground pepper
Chopped fresh parsley
Lemon wedges

Brown ground beef in medium skillet. Drain. Add okra, onions and garlic; cook 10 minutes.

Stir in broth, tomatoes, corn, parsley sprigs, bay leaf, thyme and ground red pepper. Season with salt and pepper to taste.

Bring to boil. Reduce heat to low; cover. Simmer 20 minutes or until vegetables are tender, stirring occasionally. Discard parsley sprigs and bay leaf. Ladle into bowls. Sprinkle with chopped parsley. Serve with lemon wedges.
Makes about 6 servings

Variation: Increase ground beef to 1 lb. for a main-dish soup.

One-dish meals are one easy solution to feeding the family-on-the-go. Page through this chapter for marvelous in-a-minute casseroles and other foolproof one-dish meals. This impressive assortment of quick recipe ideas will delight every member of your family.

Cheeseburger Pie

1 (9-inch) unbaked pastry shell
8 slices BORDEN® Process American Cheese Food
1 pound lean ground beef
½ cup tomato sauce
⅓ cup chopped green bell pepper
⅓ cup chopped onion
1 teaspoon WYLER'S® or STEERO® Beef-Flavor Instant Bouillon or 1 Beef-Flavor Bouillon Cube
3 eggs, beaten
2 tablespoons flour
Chopped tomato and shredded lettuce, optional

Preheat oven to 425°F. Bake pastry shell 8 minutes. Remove from oven. Reduce oven temperature to 350°F. Meanwhile, cut 6 slices cheese food into pieces. In large skillet, brown meat; pour off fat. Add tomato sauce, green pepper, onion and bouillon; cook and stir until bouillon dissolves. Remove from heat; stir in eggs, flour and cheese food pieces. Turn into prepared pastry shell. Bake 20 to 25 minutes or until hot. Arrange remaining 2 slices cheese food on top. Return to oven 3 minutes or until cheese food begins to melt. Garnish with tomato and lettuce if desired. Refrigerate leftovers.

Makes one 9-inch pie

Quick and Easy Spanish Rice and Beef

¾ pound ground beef
1 can (14½ oz.) stewed tomatoes
1 cup water
1 package (10 ounces) BIRDS EYE® Sweet Corn or Mixed Vegetables
½ teaspoon salt
½ teaspoon dried oregano leaves
½ teaspoon chili powder
¼ teaspoon garlic powder
⅛ teaspoon pepper
1½ cups MINUTE® Rice

Brown meat in large skillet. Add tomatoes, water, corn and seasonings. Bring to a boil and boil about 2 minutes. Stir in rice. Cover; remove from heat. Let stand 5 minutes. Fluff with a fork.

Makes 4 servings

Cheeseburger Pie

Pinwheel Meat Loaf

½ cup milk
1½ cups crustless Italian or French
    bread cubes
1½ pounds ground beef
½ pound sweet Italian sausage,
    removed from casings
    and crumbled
2 eggs, slightly beaten
2 tablespoons finely chopped
    parsley
1 tablespoon finely chopped
    garlic
1 teaspoon salt
½ teaspoon pepper
2 cups water
1 tablespoon butter or margarine
1 package LIPTON® Rice & Sauce
    —Cajun-Style
2 packages (10 ounces each)
    frozen chopped spinach,
    thawed and squeezed dry

In small bowl, pour milk over bread cubes, then mash with fork until bread is soaked.

In large bowl, thoroughly combine bread mixture, ground beef, sausage, eggs, parsley, garlic, salt and pepper. Place on 12×12-inch sheet of aluminum foil moistened with water. Cover with 12×14-inch sheet of waxed paper moistened with water. Using hands or rolling pin, press into 12×12-inch rectangle. Refrigerate 2 hours or until well chilled.

In medium saucepan, bring water, butter and rice & Cajun-style sauce to a boil. Continue boiling over medium heat, stirring occasionally, 10 minutes or until rice is tender. Refrigerate 2 hours or until well chilled.

Preheat oven to 350°F. Remove waxed paper from ground beef mixture. If desired, season spinach with additional salt and pepper. Spread spinach over ground beef mixture leaving 1-inch border.

Spread rice evenly over spinach. Roll, starting at long end and using foil as guide, jelly roll style, removing foil while rolling; seal edges tightly. In 13×9-inch baking pan, place meat loaf seam-side down. Bake 1 hour or until done. Let stand 15 minutes before serving. Cut into 1-inch slices.
Makes about 8 servings

Streamlined Chimichangas

This lively version of the classic Southwestern favorite shortcuts preparation with ground meat and oven baking.

1 pound ground beef or pork
1 medium onion, chopped
1 garlic clove, minced
¾ cup PACE® picante sauce
1 teaspoon ground cumin
½ teaspoon oregano leaves,
    crushed
½ teaspoon salt
8 flour tortillas (7 to 8 inches)
¼ cup melted butter
    Dairy sour cream
    Guacamole

Brown meat with onion and garlic; drain. Stir in picante sauce, cumin, oregano and salt; simmer 5 minutes or until most of liquid has evaporated. Brush 1 side of tortillas with butter; spoon heaping ⅓ cup meat mixture onto center of unbuttered sides. Fold 2 sides over filling; fold ends down. Place seam side down in 13×9×2-inch baking dish. Bake in preheated oven at 475°F. about 13 minutes or until golden brown. Top with sour cream, guacamole and additional picante sauce to serve. **Makes 4 servings**

Pinwheel Meat Loaf

Santa Fe Casserole Bake

A perfect dish to assemble ahead of time for quick-cooking later.

**1 pound lean ground beef
1 package (1.25 ounces) LAWRY'S® Taco Spices & Seasonings
2 cups chicken broth
¼ cup all-purpose flour
1 cup dairy sour cream
1 can (7 ounces) diced green chiles
1 package (11 ounces) tortilla chips
2 cups (8 ounces) grated Monterey Jack or Cheddar cheese
½ cup sliced green onions, including tops**

In medium skillet, brown ground beef, stirring, until cooked through; drain fat. Add Taco Spices & Seasonings; blend well. In small bowl, combine broth and flour. Add to meat mixture; bring to a boil to slightly thicken. Stir in sour cream and green chiles. In lightly greased 13×9×2-inch baking dish, place ½ of chips. Top with ½ of beef mixture, ½ of sauce, ½ of cheese and ½ of onions. Layer again with remaining ingredients, ending with onions. Bake in 375°F oven 20 to 25 minutes or until cheese is melted. Let stand 5 minutes before cutting.

Makes 6 servings

Hint: For additional flavor, top with guacamole.

Microwave Directions: Add 1 tablespoon IMPERIAL® Margarine. In 1-quart microwave-safe bowl, place beef. Microwave on HIGH 5 to 6 minutes or until thoroughly cooked, stirring once; drain fat. Add Taco Spices & Seasonings; blend well and set aside. In 1-quart measure, combine broth, flour and 1 tablespoon margarine.

Microwave on HIGH 5 minutes or until bubbling and thick, stirring once. Stir in sour cream and green chiles. In lightly greased 13×9×2-inch microwave-safe dish, layer as above. Cover with waxed paper and microwave on MEDIUM (50% power) 15 to 18 minutes or until cheese is melted, rotating after 7 minutes. Let stand 5 minutes before cutting.

Tasty Taco Pie

*Preparation time: 20 minutes
Baking time: 15 minutes*

**1 pound ground beef
2 8-oz. cans tomato sauce
1 1.25-oz. pkg. taco seasoning mix
1 8-oz. can PILLSBURY® Refrigerated Quick Crescent Dinner Rolls
½ lb. VELVEETA® Pasteurized Process Cheese Spread, cubed
1 cup shredded lettuce
½ cup chopped tomato
¼ cup pitted ripe olive slices**

Brown meat; drain. Stir in tomato sauce and seasoning mix; simmer 5 minutes. Unroll dough; press onto bottom and sides of ungreased 12-inch pizza pan. Prick bottom and sides with fork. Bake at 375°F, 10 to 12 minutes or until golden brown. Cover crust with meat mixture; top with process cheese spread. Continue baking until process cheese spread begins to melt. Top with remaining ingredients. Serve with sour cream if desired.

Makes 4 to 6 servings

Variation: Substitute VELVEETA® Mexican Pasteurized Process Cheese Spread with Jalapeño Pepper for Process Cheese Spread.

Microwave: Crumble meat into 1-quart microwave-safe bowl. Microwave on High 5 to 6 minutes, stirring after 3 minutes; drain. Stir into tomato sauce and seasoning mix. Microwave on High 3 minutes. Continue as directed. Serve with sour cream, if desired.

Stuffed Peppers

6 medium green peppers
  Boiling salted water
1 pound ground beef
1 small onion, chopped
1 can (8 oz.) kidney beans, drained
1 can (8 oz.) tomato paste
2½ cups water
1½ teaspoons salt
1 teaspoon sugar
¾ teaspoon chili powder
¼ teaspoon garlic salt
⅓ cup shredded cheddar cheese (optional)
1 tablespoon butter or margarine (optional)
2¼ cups MINUTE® Rice

Cut slice from top of peppers; remove seeds. Cook, uncovered, in salted water to cover peppers about 5 minutes; drain.

Brown beef and onion in large skillet. Add beans, tomato paste, ¼ cup of the water, ¾ teaspoon of the salt, the sugar, chili powder and garlic salt; mix well. Spoon into peppers and place in 13×9-inch baking dish. Add small amount of water to cover bottom of dish. Bake at 375° for 25 minutes or until peppers are tender. Sprinkle with cheese.

Meanwhile, bring remaining 2¼ cups water, ¾ teaspoon salt and the butter to a full boil in medium saucepan. Stir in rice. Cover; remove from heat. Let stand 5 minutes. Fluff with fork. Serve with peppers.   *Makes 6 servings*

Mini Meat Loaves & Vegetables

Ready to bake in just 10 easy minutes.

1½ pounds lean ground beef
1 egg
1 can (8 ounces) tomato sauce
1 can (2.8 ounces) DURKEE® French Fried Onions
½ teaspoon salt
½ teaspoon DURKEE® Italian Seasoning
6 small red potatoes, thinly sliced (about 1½ cups)
1 bag (16 ounces) frozen vegetable combination (broccoli, corn, red pepper), thawed and drained
Salt
DURKEE® Ground Black Pepper

Preheat oven to 375°F. In medium bowl, combine ground beef, egg, ½ can tomato sauce, ½ can French Fried Onions, ½ teaspoon salt and Italian seasoning. Shape into 3 mini loaves and place in 9×13-inch baking dish. Arrange potatoes around loaves. Bake, covered, at 375°F for 35 minutes. Spoon vegetables around meat loaves; stir to combine with potatoes. Lightly season vegetables with salt and pepper, if desired. Top meat loaves with remaining tomato sauce. Bake, uncovered, 15 minutes or until meat loaves are done. Top loaves with remaining onions; bake, uncovered, 3 minutes or until onions are golden brown.   *Makes 6 servings*

Microwave Directions: Prepare meat loaves as above. Arrange potatoes on bottom of 8×12-inch microwave-safe dish; place meat loaves on potatoes. Cook, covered, on HIGH 13 minutes. Rotate dish halfway through cooking time. Add vegetables and season as above. Top meat loaves with remaining tomato sauce. Cook, covered, 7 minutes or until meat loaves are done. Rotate dish halfway through cooking time. Top loaves with remaining onions; cook, uncovered, 1 minute. Let stand 5 minutes.

Patchwork Casserole

A popular, easy meat and potato casserole to carry to a potluck dinner.

2 pounds ground beef
2 cups chopped green bell pepper
1 cup chopped onion
2 pounds frozen Southern-style hash-brown potatoes, thawed
2 cans (8 ounces each) tomato sauce
1 cup water
1 can (6 ounces) tomato paste
1 teaspoon salt
½ teaspoon dried basil, crumbled
¼ teaspoon ground black pepper
1 pound pasteurized process American cheese, thinly sliced

1. Cook and stir beef in large skillet over medium heat until crumbled and brown, about 10 minutes; drain off fat.

2. Add green pepper and onion; saute until soft, about 4 minutes. Stir in all remaining ingredients except cheese.

3. Spoon ½ of the meat mixture into 13×9×2-inch baking pan or 3-quart baking dish; top with ½ of the cheese. Spoon remaining meat mixture evenly on top of cheese.

4. Cover pan with aluminum foil. Bake in preheated 350°F oven 45 minutes.

5. Cut remaining cheese into decorative shapes; place on top of casserole. Let stand, loosely covered, until cheese melts, about 5 minutes.   *Makes 8 to 10 servings*

Chopped Beef Stroganoff

1½ pounds ground beef
1 small onion, chopped
1 envelope LIPTON® Beefy Mushroom Recipe Soup Mix
2 tablespoons all-purpose flour
2 cups water
½ cup sour cream
   Hot cooked noodles (optional)

Cook and stir ground beef with onion in large skillet over medium-high heat until onion is tender. Stir in soup mix, flour and water. Bring to a boil over high heat. Reduce heat to low. Cover and simmer 10 minutes. Stir in sour cream; heat through. *Do not boil.* Serve over noodles.   *Makes about 4 servings*

Baked Spaghetti Supper

1 package (7 ounces) or ½ of 1-pound package uncooked CREAMETTE® Spaghetti
1 pound ground beef
2 tablespoons butter or margarine
¼ cup plus 1 tablespoon all-purpose flour, divided
⅔ cup instant nonfat dry milk
½ teaspoon salt
⅛ teaspoon pepper
1 envelope (1⅜ cunces) onion soup mix, divided
2 cups water
1 cup sour cream
   Buttered bread crumbs

Prepare spaghetti according to package directions; drain. Cook and stir ground beef in large skillet over medium-high heat until no longer pink. Remove with slotted spoon and set aside. Drain drippings from skillet. Melt butter over medium heat in same skillet. Stir in ¼ cup of the flour, the nonfat dry milk, salt, pepper and ½ of the soup mix. Gradually stir in water. Cook until thickened, stirring constantly. Add ground beef. Combine remaining soup mix and remaining 1 tablespoon flour in small bowl. Stir in sour cream. Combine sour cream mixture and spaghetti in large bowl, tossing to coat. Transfer spaghetti mixture into buttered 2-quart casserole, pushing spaghetti up the sides to form a well in center. Pour meat mixture into well. Top with buttered bread crumbs. Bake at 350°F 30 minutes or until heated through.   *Makes 6 to 8 servings*

Patchwork Casserole

Easy Beef Tortilla Pizzas

- 1 pound ground beef
- 1 medium onion, chopped
- 1 teaspoon dried oregano, crushed
- 1 teaspoon salt
- 4 large flour tortillas (10-inch diameter)
- 4 teaspoons olive oil
- 1 medium tomato, seeded, chopped
  Greek or Mexican Toppings (recipes follow)

Cook and stir ground beef and onion in large skillet over medium-high heat until beef loses pink color. Pour off drippings. Sprinkle oregano and salt over beef, stirring to combine. Place tortillas on 2 large baking sheets. Lightly brush surface of each tortilla with oil. Bake in preheated 400°F oven 3 minutes. Divide beef mixture evenly over tops of tortillas; divide tomato and desired topping over beef mixture. Bake at 400°F 12 to 14 minutes, rearranging baking sheets halfway through cooking time.

Makes 4 servings

Greek Topping:
Combine 1 teaspoon dried basil, crushed, ½ teaspoon lemon pepper, 4 ounces crumbled Feta cheese and ¼ cup grated Parmesan cheese in small bowl.

Mexican Topping:
Combine 1 teaspoon dried cilantro, crushed, ½ teaspoon crushed dried red chilies, 1 cup (4 ounces) shredded Monterey Jack or Cheddar cheese and ⅓ cup sliced ripe olives in small bowl.

Recipe courtesy of **National Live Stock & Meat Board**

Zucchini Lasagna

- 1½ pounds ground beef
- ¾ pound sweet Italian sausage, casing removed
- 3 tablespoons FILIPPO BERIO® Olive Oil
- 1½ cups coarsely chopped mushrooms
- 1 large onion, chopped
- 1 large clove garlic, minced
- 1 can (14½ ounces) tomatoes, chopped, undrained
- 1 jar (15 ounces) marinara sauce
- 1 teaspoon salt
- 1 teaspoon dried basil, crushed
- ½ teaspoon Italian herb seasoning
- 1 container (24 ounces) ricotta cheese
- 1 package (8 ounces) mozzarella cheese, cubed, divided
- ¼ cup chopped Italian parsley
- 2 eggs, beaten
- 6 unpeeled zucchini, cut lengthwise into thin slices about 8 inches long

Cook beef and sausage in hot oil in large skillet over medium-high heat until meats are no longer pink. Add mushrooms, onion and garlic. Cook several minutes, stirring frequently. Add tomatoes, marinara sauce, salt, basil and Italian seasoning. Combine ricotta, ¾ of the mozzarella, the parsley and eggs in medium bowl. Spoon 1 cup of the sauce onto bottom of 13×9-inch baking dish. Top with ⅓ of the zucchini, ⅓ of the cheese mixture and then 1 cup of the sauce. Repeat layers, ending with sauce. Cover with foil. Bake at 350°F 45 minutes. Sprinkle with remaining mozzarella. Bake, uncovered, 10 minutes more or until cheese melts. Let stand 10 minutes before cutting. Heat remaining sauce and serve with lasagna.

Makes 8 servings

Easy Beef Tortilla Pizzas

Classic Hamburger Casserole

Ready to bake in just 10 easy minutes.

- 2 cups hot mashed potatoes
- 1 pound ground beef
- 1 package (9 ounces) frozen cut green beans, thawed and drained
- 1 can (10¾ ounces) condensed tomato soup
- ¼ cup water
- ½ teaspoon DURKEE® Seasoned Salt
- ⅛ teaspoon DURKEE® Ground Black Pepper
- 1 can (2.8 ounces) DURKEE® French Fried Onions
- ½ cup (2 ounces) shredded Cheddar cheese

Preheat oven to 350°F. In medium skillet, brown ground beef; drain. Stir in green beans, soup, water and seasonings; pour into 1½-quart casserole. In medium bowl, combine mashed potatoes and ½ can French Fried Onions. Spoon potato mixture in mounds around edge of the casserole. Bake, uncovered, at 350°F for 25 minutes or until heated through. Top potatoes with cheese and remaining onions; bake, uncovered, 5 minutes or until onions are golden brown.

Makes 4 to 6 servings

Kansas City Vegetable Soup

- 1 pound lean ground beef
- 1 cup chopped onion
- 2 cloves garlic, finely chopped
- 6 cups water
- 1 (28-ounce) can tomatoes, undrained
- 2 tablespoons WYLER'S® or STEERO® Instant Bouillon *or* 6 Beef-Flavor Bouillon Cubes
- ¼ to ½ teaspoon pepper
- 2 cups frozen hash brown potatoes
- 1 cup frozen peas and carrots
  Sour cream and chopped parsley, optional

In Dutch oven or large kettle, brown meat with onion and garlic; pour off fat. Add water, tomatoes, bouillon and pepper. Bring to a boil; reduce heat and simmer uncovered 20 minutes. Stir in potatoes and peas and carrots; cook uncovered 15 minutes longer or until vegetables are tender. Serve with sour cream and parsley if desired. Refrigerate leftovers. *Makes about 2½ quarts*

Nachos Casserole

- 1 cup chunky taco sauce
- 1 can (4 ounces) chopped green chilies, drained
- 1 pound ground beef
- ½ cup chopped onion
- ¼ teaspoon ground cumin
- 2 cups (8 ounces) shredded Cheddar cheese, divided
- 1 cup refried beans
- ½ cup water
- 4 cups KELLOGG'S® CORN FLAKES® cereal, divided
  Chopped tomatoes
  Sour cream
  Chopped green onions
  Sliced pitted ripe olives

Combine taco sauce and chilies in small bowl; set aside. Cook and stir ground beef and onion in large skillet over medium-high heat until meat is no longer pink; drain. Add cumin, 1 cup of the cheese, the beans, ½ of the taco sauce mixture and the water. Pour 2 cups of the cereal into lightly buttered 12×8-inch glass baking dish. Cover with meat mixture. Top with remaining taco sauce mixture. Sprinkle with remaining 2 cups cereal. Bake at 350°F 25 minutes or until heated through. Sprinkle with remaining 1 cup cheese. Bake just until cheese melts. Garnish with tomatoes, sour cream, green onions and sliced olives.

Makes 6 servings

Hearty Beef 'n Vegetables

Ready to bake in just 15 easy minutes.

4 cups frozen potato rounds
1 pound ground beef
1 package (10 ounces) frozen chopped broccoli, thawed and drained
1 can (2.8 ounces) DURKEE® French Fried Onions
1 medium tomato, chopped (optional)
1 can (10¾ ounces) condensed cream of celery soup
⅓ cup milk
1 cup (4 ounces) shredded Cheddar cheese
¼ teaspoon DURKEE® Garlic Powder
⅛ teaspoon DURKEE® Ground Black Pepper

Preheat oven to 400°F. Arrange frozen potatoes in bottom and up sides of 8×12-inch baking dish to form a shell. Bake, uncovered, at 400°F for 10 minutes. In medium skillet, brown ground beef, leaving in large chunks; drain well. Layer beef, broccoli, ½ can French Fried Onions and the tomato in potato shell. In small bowl, combine soup, milk, ½ cup cheese and the seasonings; pour evenly over beef mixture. Bake, covered, at 400°F for 20 minutes or until heated through. Top with remaining cheese and onions; bake, uncovered, 1 to 3 minutes or until onions are golden brown. *Makes 4 to 6 servings*

Microwave Directions: In 8×12-inch microwave-safe dish, arrange potatoes as above; set aside. Crumble ground beef into large microwave-safe bowl. Cook, covered, on High 4 to 6 minutes or until beef is cooked. Stir beef halfway through cooking time. Drain well. Stir in broccoli, ½ can onions, the soup, milk, ½ cup cheese and the seasonings. Cook, covered, 6 minutes, stirring beef mixture halfway through cooking time. Stir tomato into beef mixture; spoon into potato shell. Cook, covered, 8 minutes or until heated through. Rotate dish halfway through cooking time. Top with remaining cheese and onions; cook, uncovered, 1 minute or until cheese melts. Let stand 5 minutes.

Beef and Wild Rice Casserole

2⅔ cups boiling water
⅔ cup uncooked wild rice, rinsed and drained
4 teaspoons WYLER'S® or STEERO® Beef-Flavor Instant Bouillon *or* 4 Beef-Flavor Bouillon Cubes
1½ pounds lean ground beef
1 cup chopped celery
½ cup chopped onion
1 clove garlic, finely chopped
1 10¾-ounce can condensed cream of mushroom soup
½ cup uncooked long grain rice
⅛ teaspoon pepper

Preheat oven to 350°. In 2-quart baking dish, combine water, wild rice and bouillon; set aside. In large skillet, brown meat; pour off fat. Stir in celery, onion and garlic; cook until tender. Add remaining ingredients. Stir meat mixture into wild rice mixture; mix well. Cover. Bake 1 hour and 30 minutes. Serve hot. Refrigerate leftovers.

Makes 8 servings

INTERNATIONAL FLAIR

Experience exotic flavors from around the world! These tantalizing recipes are inspired by countries spanning the globe. Choose from spicy Middle Eastern Stuffed Squash, traditional Borscht with Meatballs, slightly sweet Caribbean Cheese & Beef Casserole and many more. Your taste buds will be delightfully awakened by these wonderful new taste sensations.

Meat-Filled Oriental Pancakes

6 Oriental Pancakes (recipe follows)
1 tablespoon cornstarch
3 tablespoons KIKKOMAN® Soy Sauce
1 tablespoon dry sherry
¾ pound ground beef
½ pound ground pork
⅔ cup chopped green onions and tops
1 teaspoon minced fresh ginger root
1 clove garlic, pressed

Prepare Oriental Pancakes. Combine cornstarch, soy sauce and sherry in large bowl. Add beef, pork, green onions, ginger and garlic; mix until thoroughly combined. Spread ½ cup meat mixture evenly over each pancake, leaving about a ½-inch border on 1 side. Starting with opposite side, roll up pancake jelly-roll fashion. Place rolls, seam sides down, in single layer on heatproof plate; place plate on steamer rack. Set rack in large pot or wok of boiling water. Cover and steam 15 minutes. (For best results, steam all rolls at the same time.) Just before serving, cut rolls diagonally into quarters. Arrange on serving platter and serve hot.

Makes 2 dozen appetizers

Oriental Pancakes:
Beat *4 eggs* in large bowl with wire whisk. Combine *½ cup water*, *3 tablespoons cornstarch*, *2 teaspoons KIKKOMAN® Soy Sauce* and *½ teaspoon sugar*; pour into eggs and beat well. Heat an 8-inch omelet or crepe pan over medium heat. Brush bottom of pan with *½ teaspoon vegetable oil*; reduce heat to low. Beat egg mixture; pour ¼ cupful into skillet, lifting and tipping pan from side to side to form a thin round pancake. Cook around 1 to 1½ minutes, or until firm. Carefully lift with spatula and transfer to a sheet of waxed paper. Continue procedure, adding ½ *teaspoon oil* to pan for each pancake.

Makes 6 pancakes

Meat-Filled Oriental Pancakes

Meat Loaf Olé

Turn a family favorite into a Mexican fiesta.

- 1½ pounds lean ground beef
- ¾ cup unseasoned dry bread crumbs
- 1 egg, beaten
- 1 can (4 ounces) diced green chiles
- ½ cup (2 ounces) grated Cheddar cheese
- 1 package (1.25 ounces) LAWRY'S® Taco Spices & Seasonings
- 1 medium tomato, chopped
- ½ cup sliced green onions
- 2 tablespoons ketchup
- 1 tablespoon salsa
- ½ teaspoon LAWRY'S® Seasoned Salt

In large bowl, combine ground beef, bread crumbs, egg, chiles, Cheddar cheese and Taco Spices & Seasonings; blend well. Pat meat mixture into 9×5×3-inch loaf pan. Bake, uncovered, in 350°F oven about 1 hour or until meat is cooked through. Let stand 10 minutes before draining fat and removing meat loaf from pan. In small bowl, combine remaining ingredients. Slice meat loaf into ½-inch slices and spoon tomato mixture over slices.

Makes 6 servings

Presentation: Serve with Mexican rice.

Hungarian Beef Rolls

- Spicy Tomato Sauce (recipe follows)
- 4 bacon slices, finely chopped
- ½ cup finely chopped onion
- 1 small garlic clove, minced
- ¾ lb. lean ground beef
- 2 eggs, beaten
- Salt
- Dash of freshly ground pepper
- 1 tablespoon paprika, Hungarian if possible
- 1½ pounds beef top round, sliced ½ inch thick (about 12 slices)
- 2 tablespoons vegetable oil

Prepare Spicy Tomato Sauce; keep warm while preparing beef rolls.

Cook bacon in medium skillet until partially cooked. Add onion and garlic; continue cooking until bacon is crisp and onion is tender. Drain.

Combine bacon mixture, ground beef, eggs and seasonings in medium bowl; mix lightly. Set aside.

Pound each beef slice to ¼-inch thickness. Spoon approximately 2 tablespoons ground beef mixture onto one end of each beef slice; roll to enclose filling. Secure with wooden pick or tie closed with kitchen string. Repeat with remaining beef slices and ground beef mixture.

Heat oil in large skillet. Add beef rolls in batches; cook until browned on all sides.

Add to Spicy Tomato Sauce; bring to boil. Reduce heat; cover. Simmer 50 minutes or until beef is tender. Remove wooden picks before serving.

Spicy Tomato Sauce

- 1 tablespoon vegetable oil
- 1 medium onion, chopped
- 1 garlic clove, minced
- 1 can (14½ ounces) tomatoes, crushed
- 2 cups chicken broth
- 2 tablespoons tomato paste
- 1 teaspoon paprika, Hungarian if possible
- Bay leaves
- ½ teaspoon salt
- Dash of freshly ground pepper

Heat oil in a large saucepan. Add onion and garlic; cook until tender. Stir in remaining ingredients. Bring to boil. Reduce heat; simmer until ready to serve. Remove bay leaves just before serving.

Makes 6 servings

Pastitsio
(Greek Macaroni Bake)

Pasta layer:
- 1 (7-ounce) package or 2 cups CREAMETTES® Elbow Macaroni, cooked and drained
- 2 eggs, beaten
- 1/3 cup grated Parmesan cheese
- 1 tablespoon margarine or butter, melted

Meat layer:
- 1 pound lean ground beef
- 1/2 cup finely chopped onion
- 1 clove garlic, finely chopped
- 1 (8-ounce) can tomato sauce
- 1/4 teaspoon ground allspice
- 1/4 teaspoon ground cinnamon
- 1/4 teaspoon ground nutmeg
- 2 teaspoons WYLER'S® or STEERO® Beef-Flavor Instant Bouillon or 2 Beef-Flavor Bouillon Cubes
- 1/8 teaspoon pepper

Cream sauce:
- 3 tablespoons margarine or butter
- 2 tablespoons flour
- 1 teaspoon WYLER'S® or STEERO® Chicken-Flavor Instant Bouillon or 1 Chicken-Flavor Bouillon Cube
- 1/8 teaspoon pepper
- 2 cups BORDEN® or MEADOW GOLD® Milk
- 1/4 cup grated Parmesan cheese

In large bowl, stir together macaroni, eggs, 1/3 cup Parmesan cheese and 1 tablespoon melted margarine. Spoon evenly into greased 3-quart shallow baking dish (13×9-inch). In large skillet, brown meat; pour off fat. Stir in onion and garlic; cook and stir until onion is tender. Add tomato sauce, allspice, cinnamon, nutmeg, 2 teaspoons beef bouillon and pepper; mix well. Simmer 10 minutes. Spoon evenly over macaroni mixture. In medium saucepan, melt 3 tablespoons margarine; stir in flour, 1 teaspoon chicken bouillon and pepper.

Gradually stir in milk. Cook and stir over medium heat until slightly thickened (mixture should coat spoon). Remove from heat. Stir in remaining 1/4 cup Parmesan cheese. Spoon evenly over meat layer. Cover. Bake in preheated 325° oven 30 minutes or until bubbly. Garnish as desired. Refrigerate leftovers.

Buenos Burritos

To serve "dry," place all ingredients on tortillas before rolling. To serve "wet," fill with meat and cheese, roll and top with remaining ingredients.

- 12 flour tortillas (7- to 8-inch diameter), heated*
- Picante Meat Filling (recipe follows)
- 4 cups (16 ounces) shredded monterey jack or cheddar cheese
- Shredded lettuce
- Dairy sour cream
- PACE® picante sauce

For each burrito, spoon scant 1/4 cup Picante Meat Filling down center of tortilla; top with 2 heaping tablespoonfuls cheese. Add lettuce, sour cream and picante sauce, as desired. Fold tortilla over one end of filling; roll. **Makes 6 servings**

*To heat tortillas, stack and wrap securely in foil; place in 350°F. oven about 15 minutes. Or, wrap loosely in plastic wrap and cook in microwave oven at HIGH for 1/2 to 1 minute.

Picante Meat Filling

Interchangeable in tacos, tostadas and burritos, this easy filling can be doubled, made ahead and refrigerated or frozen and reheated.

- 1 pound ground beef
- 1 small onion, chopped
- 1 garlic clove, minced
- 3/4 cup PACE® picante sauce
- 1 teaspoon ground cumin
- 1/2 teaspoon salt

Brown meat with onion and garlic; drain. Stir in remaining ingredients; simmer 5 minutes or until most of the liquid has evaporated.

Makes 4 to 6 servings

Mexican Stuffed Shells

Ready to bake in just 15 easy minutes.

12 pasta stuffing shells, cooked in unsalted water and drained
1 pound ground beef
1 jar (12 ounces) mild or medium picante sauce
½ cup water
1 can (8 ounces) tomato sauce
1 can (4 ounces) chopped green chilies, drained
1 cup (4 ounces) shredded Monterey Jack cheese
1 can (2.8 ounces) DURKEE® French Fried Onions

Preheat oven to 350°F. In large skillet, brown ground beef; drain. In small bowl, combine picante sauce, water and tomato sauce. Stir ½ *cup* sauce mixture into beef along with chilies, ½ *cup* cheese and ½ *can* French Fried Onions; mix well. Spread *half* the remaining sauce mixture in bottom of 10-inch round baking dish. Stuff cooked shells with beef mixture. Arrange shells in baking dish; top with remaining sauce. Bake, covered, at 350° for 30 minutes or until heated through. Top with remaining onions and cheese; bake, uncovered, 5 minutes or until cheese is melted.

Makes 6 servings

Microwave Directions: Crumble ground beef into medium microwave-safe bowl. Cook, covered, on HIGH 4 to 6 minutes or until beef is cooked. Stir beef halfway through cooking time. Drain well. Prepare sauce mixture as above; spread ½ *cup* in 8×12-inch microwave-safe dish. Prepare beef mixture as above. Stuff cooked shells with beef mixture. Arrange shells in dish; top with remaining sauce. Cook, covered, 10 to 12 minutes or until heated through. Rotate dish halfway through cooking time. Top with remaining onions and cheese; cook, uncovered, 1 minute or until cheese is melted. Let stand 5 minutes.

Middle Eastern Stuffed Squash

1 pound lean ground beef
½ cup cooked rice
½ cup finely chopped onion
1 egg, beaten
2 tablespoons chopped parsley
2 teaspoons finely chopped fresh mint or 1 teaspoon dried leaf mint
1 teaspoon salt
½ teaspoon ground allspice
¼ teaspoon ground cumin
Freshly ground pepper
8 medium zucchini
2 tablespoons olive oil
1 can (14½ ounces) tomatoes, chopped, undrained
½ cup cold water
Dash of hot pepper sauce
1 marjoram sprig or ¼ teaspoon dried leaf marjoram

Combine ground beef, rice, ¼ cup onion, egg, parsley, mint and seasonings in medium bowl; mix lightly. Set aside.

Cut ends off zucchini; cut zucchini in half crosswise. Hollow out centers of zucchini, leaving ¼-inch-thick shell. Fill shells with ground beef mixture, smoothing ends.

Saute remaining ¼ cup onion in olive oil in large skillet with lid. Add tomatoes, water, hot pepper sauce and marjoram. Bring to a boil; reduce heat to low. Place zucchini in tomato mixture. Cover; simmer 25 minutes or until zucchini is tender when pierced with fork. Spoon sauce over zucchini to serve.

Makes 8 servings

Variation: Substitute sixteen small pattypan squash for eight zucchini.

Tip: Use apple corer to hollow out zucchini.

Tacos Suave de Carne con Salsa Roja

¾ cup vegetable oil
1 tablespoon pure ground chile pepper*
1 pound ground beef
2 teaspoons ground cumin
1 tablespoon Chef Paul Prudhomme's SEAFOOD MAGIC®
1 tablespoon Chef Paul Prudhomme's MEAT MAGIC®
1 cup chopped onion
½ cup chopped green bell pepper
3 tablespoons corn flour or all-purpose flour
1½ cups beef stock or water
12 (6-inch) corn tortillas
    Shredded lettuce
    Chopped fresh tomatoes
    Shredded Cheddar cheese

Heat ¼ cup of the oil in heavy 10-inch skillet over high heat 1 minute. Stir in chile pepper and cook 1½ minutes, stirring frequently. Add ground beef and cumin. Cook, stirring frequently, to break up meat chunks, about 2 minutes. Add SEAFOOD MAGIC® and MEAT MAGIC® and stir to mix well. Cook 1 minute more. Add onion and bell pepper. Cook 6 minutes, stirring occasionally, or until meat is well browned. Stir in flour. Cook, without stirring, about 2 minutes or until a brown crust forms on bottom of pan. Stir in stock to deglaze pan, stirring and scraping pan bottom well to get up all browned bits. Cook about 3 minutes or until sauce is boiling. Reduce heat to low and simmer about 8 minutes or until sauce has reduced somewhat and flavors have blended. Turn heat off.

In 8-inch skillet, heat the remaining oil over high heat about 3 minutes or until it reaches 300°F. Slide 1 tortilla into hot oil and, using tongs, immediately turn tortilla over and then immediately pull it out of pan. Tortilla should be very soft and pliable. Drain on paper towels. Repeat with the remaining tortillas. Blot any of the remaining oil with fresh paper towels.

To assemble, lay tortillas on serving plates, allowing 2 per person. Spoon ¼ cup meat mixture over half of each tortilla. Top with lettuce, tomatoes and cheese. Fold each half over filling. Serve immediately.
Makes 6 servings

*You can find pure ground chile pepper (ground dried chiles) in a Mexican or Latin grocery store. However, if you cannot find it, substitute an equal amount of chili powder.

Copyright © 1988 by Paul Prudhomme

Simply Super Sukiyaki

1 block tofu
½ cup KIKKOMAN® Soy Sauce
½ cup water
2 tablespoons sugar
¾ pound ground beef
1 medium-size yellow onion, thinly sliced
1 pound fresh spinach, trimmed, washed and drained
1 bunch green onions and tops, cut into 2-inch lengths separating whites from tops
¼ pound fresh mushrooms, sliced

Cut tofu into 1-inch cubes; drain well on several layers of paper towels. Meanwhile, combine soy sauce, water and sugar; set aside. Brown beef in Dutch oven or large skillet over medium heat, stirring to break beef into large chunks. Add yellow onion; cook 1 minute. Add spinach, white parts of green onions, mushrooms and soy sauce mixture; cook until spinach wilts, stirring constantly. Gently stir in tofu and green onion tops. Cook 5 to 7 minutes, or until vegetables are tender and tofu is seasoned with sauce. *Makes 4 to 6 servings*

Tacos Suave de Carne con Salsa Roja

Lasagna with White and Red Sauces

Béchamel Sauce (recipe
    follows)
½ medium onion, sliced
1 clove garlic, minced
2 to 3 tablespoons vegetable oil
1 pound lean ground beef
1 can (28 ounces) crushed
    tomatoes or 1 can (28 ounces)
    whole tomatoes, chopped,
    undrained
½ cup thinly sliced celery
½ cup thinly sliced carrot
1 teaspoon dried basil, crushed
1 package (1 pound) lasagna
    noodles, cooked, drained
6 ounces BEL PAESE® cheese,*
    thinly sliced
6 hard-cooked eggs, sliced
    (optional)
2 tablespoons butter or
    margarine, cut into small
    pieces
1 cup (about 2 ounces) freshly
    grated Parmigiano-Reggiano
    or Grana Padano cheese

Prepare Béchamel Sauce; set aside. Cook and stir onion and garlic in hot oil in Dutch oven over medium-high heat until tender. Add ground beef and cook until no longer pink, stirring occasionally. Add tomatoes, celery, carrot and basil. Reduce heat to low. Cover and simmer 45 minutes. Remove cover and simmer 15 minutes more.

Arrange 1/3 of the lasagna noodles in bottom of buttered 13×9-inch baking dish. Add ½ of the BEL PAESE® and ½ of the eggs. Spread with meat sauce. Repeat layers of noodles, BEL PAESE® and eggs. Spread with Béchamel Sauce. Top with layer of noodles. Dot with butter. Sprinkle with Parmigiana-Reggiano. Bake in preheated 350°F oven 30 to 40 minutes or until heated through. Let stand 10 minutes before cutting.

Makes 6 servings

*Remove wax coating and moist, white crust from cheese.

Béchamel Sauce:

Melt 2 tablespoons butter or margarine in small saucepan over medium-low heat. Stir in 2 tablespoons all-purpose flour. Gradually blend in ¾ cup milk. Season to taste with white pepper. Cook until thick and bubbly, stirring constantly. *Makes ¾ cup sauce*

Bobotie

Serve this South African dish with a tossed green salad and hot cooked rice for an easy complete meal.

1 bread slice, torn into small
    pieces
1 cup milk
1 pound ground beef
1 medium onion, chopped
2 tablespoons brown sugar
2 tablespoons white wine vinegar
1 tablespoon curry powder
    Salt and freshly ground pepper
2 medium tomatoes, chopped
1 small apple, finely chopped
½ cup raisins
⅓ cup slivered almonds
2 eggs, beaten
½ teaspoon grated lemon peel
    (optional)
4 to 6 lemon slices
4 to 6 bay leaves

Preheat oven to 350°F. Soak bread in milk in small bowl.

Brown ground beef in medium skillet. Drain. Add onions; cook until tender. Add sugar, vinegar and curry powder; mix well. Season with salt and pepper to taste. Stir in tomatoes, apples, raisins and almonds.

Squeeze milk from bread, reserving milk. Add bread to ground beef mixture; mix lightly. Spoon into greased shallow 2-quart casserole dish.

Bake 30 minutes.

Beat eggs with reserved milk and peel. Pour over ground beef mixture. Top with lemon slices and bay leaves.

Continue baking 20 minutes or until egg mixture is set. Remove bay leaves before serving.

Makes 4 to 6 servings

Lasagna with White and Red Sauces

Borscht with Meatballs

Preparation time: 10 minutes
Cooking time: 19½ to 22½ minutes

1 pound ground beef (80% lean)
1 teaspoon dill weed, divided
½ teaspoon salt
¼ teaspoon pepper, divided
2½ cups ready-to-serve beef broth
1 can (16 ounces) whole beets, undrained and quartered
2 cups finely shredded cabbage
1 medium onion, chopped
2 tablespoons fresh lemon juice
¼ cup plain yogurt (optional)

Combine ground beef, ½ teaspoon of the dill weed, the salt and ⅛ teaspoon of the pepper, mixing lightly but thoroughly. Pinch off 1½-inch pieces of beef mixture to make about 20 free-form meatballs; place around sides of 11¾×7½-inch microwave-safe dish. Cover with waxed paper. Microwave at HIGH 2½ to 3 minutes; reserve. (Meatballs may appear undercooked.) Combine broth, beets with liquid, cabbage, onion, remaining ½ teaspoon dill weed and ⅛ teaspoon pepper in 3-quart microwave-safe casserole. Cover with lid or vented plastic wrap; microwave at HIGH 15 to 17 minutes or until hot, stirring halfway through cooking time. Add meatballs and any accumulated liquid. Cover; microwave at HIGH 2 to 2½ minutes or until heated through. Stir in lemon juice. Serve with yogurt, if desired. ***Makes 4 servings***

Recipe courtesy of **National Live Stock & Meat Board**

Cantonese Meatballs

1 can (20 oz.) pineapple chunks in syrup
3 tablespoons brown sugar, packed
5 tablespoons KIKKOMAN® Teriyaki Sauce, divided
1 tablespoon vinegar
1 tablespoon tomato catsup
1 pound lean ground beef
2 tablespoons instant minced onion
2 tablespoons cornstarch
¼ cup water

Drain pineapple; reserve syrup. Combine syrup, brown sugar, 3 tablespoons teriyaki sauce, vinegar and catsup; set aside. Mix beef with remaining 2 tablespoons teriyaki sauce and onion; shape into 20 meatballs. Brown meatballs in large skillet; drain off excess fat. Pour syrup mixture over meatballs; simmer 10 minutes, stirring occasionally. Dissolve cornstarch in water; stir into skillet with pineapple. Cook and stir until sauce thickens and pineapple is heated through.

Makes 6 to 8 appetizer servings

Caribbean Cheese & Beef Casserole

The cheese is the Dutch influence, but the sweet, hot filling is pure Caribbean.

1 pound ground beef
1 small onion, chopped
1 small green pepper, chopped
1 medium tomato, chopped
2 eggs, beaten
¼ cup fresh bread crumbs
¼ cup raisins
¼ cup chopped pimiento-stuffed olives
2 tablespoons pickle relish
1 tablespoon finely chopped jalapeño pepper
½ teaspoon salt
Dash of freshly ground black pepper
12 ounces Edam cheese

Preheat oven to 350°.

Brown ground beef in medium skillet. Drain. Add onions and green peppers; cook until tender. Stir in all remaining ingredients except cheese.

Shred one-third of cheese; thinly slice remaining cheese. Add shredded cheese to ground beef mixture; spoon into greased 2-quart casserole. Arrange cheese slices on top of ground beef mixture; cover.

Bake 30 minutes or until mixture is set and cheese is melted. Let stand 5 minutes before serving.

Makes 4 to 6 servings

Borscht with Meatballs

Spark up your repertoire of outdoor grilling recipes with this irresistible collection of grilled burgers. Even burger connoisseurs will be impressed with this diverse sampling. There's everything from delicately seasoned burgers to giant, juicy stuffed burgers.

Burgers Pacific

Grilled Hawaiian pineapple tops these ginger-flavored burgers.

1½ **pounds ground beef**
⅓ **cup chopped green onions**
½ **teaspoon ground ginger**
⅛ **teaspoon pepper**
⅓ **cup apricot preserves**
⅓ **cup OPEN PIT® Original Flavor Barbecue Sauce**
6 **pineapple slices**
6 **hamburger buns, split and toasted**

1. In large bowl, combine beef, onions, ginger and pepper. Shape into six 1-inch-thick patties.

2. To make sauce: In small saucepan, combine preserves and barbecue sauce. Over medium heat, heat to boiling, stirring often.

3. On grill rack, place filled patties directly above medium coals. Grill, uncovered, until desired doneness (allow 10 minutes for medium and 12 minutes for well-done), turning and brushing often with sauce. Place pineapple on grill; grill 1 minute or until browned, turning once.

4. To serve: Place patties on buns with pineapple.   *Makes 6 servings*

To broil: Arrange patties on rack in broiler pan. Broil 4 inches from heat until desired doneness (allow 15 minutes for medium and 18 minutes for well-done), turning and brushing often with sauce. Broil pineapple 1 minute, turning once.

Spicy Taco Burgers

Chiles and cheese team up to make each new bite a surprise.

1½ **pounds lean ground beef**
1 **package (1.25 ounces) LAWRY'S® Taco Spices & Seasonings**
3 **tablespoons chili sauce or ketchup**
1 **cup (4 ounces) grated Monterey Jack cheese**
3 **tablespoons diced green chiles**
6 **Cheddar cheese slices**
6 **tomato slices**
6 **flour tortillas, warmed**

In medium bowl, combine ground beef, Taco Spices & Seasonings and chili sauce; blend well. Form into 12 patties. Sprinkle 6 of the patties with Monterey Jack cheese and green chiles. Top with remaining 6 patties, sealing around edges so cheese does not leak out. Grill or broil burgers 5 to 7 minutes on each side. Top with Cheddar cheese. Place 1 patty and 1 tomato slice near upper edge of each tortilla. Fold in sides and fold bottom half of tortilla up over burger. Secure with toothpicks.   *Makes 6 servings*

Presentation: Serve with guacamole, dairy sour cream and fresh salsa.

Burgers Pacific

Grande Beef Burger

Preparation time: 40 minutes
Cooking time: 14 minutes

Guacamole (recipe follows)
2 pounds ground beef (80% lean)
1 teaspoon each ground cumin
and salt
1 can (4 ounces) chopped green
chilies, drained
3 ounces Monterey Jack cheese,
cut into 6 slices
1 round loaf sourdough bread
(about 1½ pounds)
2 tablespoons butter, softened
1 cup shredded lettuce
1 small tomato, chopped
2 green onions with tops,
thinly sliced
2 tablespoons sliced pitted
ripe olives
½ cup dairy sour cream

Prepare Guacamole; reserve. Combine ground beef, cumin and salt, mixing lightly but thoroughly. Line 9-inch round pan with plastic wrap or aluminum foil. Divide beef mixture into 2 equal portions; shape 1 portion into large patty by pressing meat lightly but firmly into pan. Remove patty; place on lightly greased flat baking sheet. Sprinkle chilies evenly over patty; arrange cheese over chilies. Shape remaining beef mixture into large patty; place on first patty. Press edges together securely to seal.

Place burger on grid over *medium-hot* coals. Cover cooker; grill 7 minutes. To turn, slide lightly greased flat baking sheet under burger. Hold another flat baking sheet over burger; flip over and carefully slide uncooked side back onto grid. Continue grilling, covered, 7 minutes or to desired doneness. Remove burger from grid with flat baking sheet. Meanwhile, slice loaf horizontally in half to form bun. Remove soft bread from inside top half of bun, leaving ½- to 1-inch thick shell. Spread cut sides of bun with butter; toast cut sides on grid

1 minute. Place burger on bottom half of bun. Arrange lettuce, tomato, green onions and olives on top of burger; cover with top of bun. Cut into wedges. Serve Guacamole and sour cream with burger.

Makes 8 servings

Note: If using an open grill, increase cooking time 3 minutes.

Guacamole

1 large avocado, peeled,
seeded and cut into pieces
1 small onion, quartered
2 teaspoons fresh lemon juice
1 teaspoon Worcestershire sauce
¼ teaspoon each hot pepper
sauce, salt and sugar

Place all ingredients in food processor bowl fitted with steel knife or in blender container. Process until mixture is blended. Cover; refrigerate until ready to serve.

Recipe courtesy of **National Live Stock & Meat Board**

Pizza Burgers

1 pound lean ground beef
1 cup (4 ounces) shredded
mozzarella cheese
1 tablespoon minced onion
1½ teaspoons chopped fresh
oregano or ½ teaspoon dried
leaf oregano
1 tablespoon chopped fresh basil
or 1 teaspoon dried leaf basil
½ teaspoon salt
Dash of freshly ground pepper
Prepared pizza sauce, heated
English muffins

Preheat grill.

Combine ground beef, cheese, onions and seasonings in medium bowl; mix lightly. Shape into four patties.

Grill 8 minutes or to desired doneness, turning once. Top with pizza sauce. Serve on English muffins. *Makes 4 servings*

Grilled Beef with Creamy Jalapeño Sauce

2 egg yolks
1 to 1½ teaspoons chopped fresh or canned jalapeño peppers
1 tablespoon coarsely chopped cilantro
2 tablespoons lemon juice
¾ cup butter, melted and warm
2 to 3 drops hot pepper sauce
6 ground beef patties, about 1 inch thick
Salt
Ground black pepper
3 tomatoes, sliced, for garnish
Cilantro sprigs for garnish

To prepare sauce, process egg yolks, jalapeño peppers and chopped cilantro in blender container until seasonings are finely chopped. Heat lemon juice in small pan to simmering. Add to egg yolk mixture; blend 45 seconds. With motor on medium speed, add butter, a few drops at a time in the beginning but increase to a thin, regular stream as mixture begins to thicken. (Sauce will be consistency of a creamy salad dressing.) Stir in hot pepper sauce. Pour into jar; cover. Refrigerate until ready to use. While meat is cooking, heat sauce over low heat until warm.

Preheat charcoal grill and grease grill rack. Place meat on grill 4 to 6 inches above solid bed of coals (coals should be evenly covered with gray ashes). Cook, turning once, 3 to 5 minutes on each side for rare or to desired doneness. Season with salt and black pepper to taste. Spoon sauce over meat; garnish with tomato slices and cilantro sprigs.   ***Makes 6 servings***

Heartland Burgers

Serve these with VLASIC® Kosher Dill Spears and Chips.

1 pound ground beef
1 cup thinly sliced mushrooms
¼ cup finely chopped onion
½ teaspoon Worcestershire sauce
¼ teaspoon salt
Generous dash pepper
⅓ cup OPEN PIT® Original Flavor Barbecue Sauce
4 whole wheat hamburger buns, split, toasted and buttered
Lettuce leaves
Tomato slices
VLASIC® Hamburger Relish
Sliced onion

In large bowl, combine beef, mushrooms, chopped onion, Worcestershire, salt and pepper. Shape into four 1-inch-thick patties.

On grill rack, place patties directly above medium coals. Grill, uncovered, until desired doneness (allow 10 minutes for medium and 12 minutes for well-done), turning and brushing often with barbecue sauce. Place patties on buns with lettuce, tomato, relish and sliced onion.   ***Makes 4 servings***

To broil: Arrange patties on rack in broiler pan. Broil 4 inches from heat until desired doneness (allow 15 minutes for medium and 18 minutes for well-done), turning and brushing often with barbecue sauce.

GREAT GRILLED BURGERS

Two-Way Burgers

Prepare Grilled Burgers and choose one of two different burger recipes—California Burgers or English Burgers.

*Grilled Burgers

Preparation time: 10 minutes
Cooking time: 10 to 12 minutes

1 pound ground beef
¼ cup minced onion
¼ teaspoon pepper

Combine ground beef, onion and pepper, mixing lightly but thoroughly. Divide beef mixture into 4 equal portions and form into patties 4 inches in diameter. Broil patties on grid over medium coals, turning once. Broil 10 minutes for rare; 12 minutes for medium. Prepare recipe desired and assemble as directed.   *4 beef patties*

California Burgers

Preparation time: 15 minutes

1 recipe Grilled Burgers*
¼ cup plain yogurt
1 teaspoon Dijon-style mustard
4 whole wheat hamburger buns, split
12 large spinach leaves, stems removed
4 thin slices red onion
4 large mushrooms, sliced
1 small avocado, peeled, seeded and cut into 12 wedges

Combine yogurt and mustard. On bottom half of each bun, layer an equal amount of spinach leaves, onions and mushrooms; top each with a Grilled Burger. Arrange 3 avocado wedges on each patty; top with an equal amount of yogurt mixture. Close each sandwich with bun top.   *4 servings*

English Burgers

Preparation time: 15 minutes

1 recipe Grilled Burgers*
¼ cup each horseradish sauce and chopped tomato
2 tablespoons crumbled crisply cooked bacon
4 English muffins, split, lightly toasted

Combine horseradish sauce, tomato and bacon. Place a Grilled Burger on each muffin half. Spoon an equal amount of horseradish sauce mixture over each patty. Cover with remaining muffin half.
          4 servings

Note: One tablespoon canned real bacon bits may be substituted for cooked bacon.

Recipe courtesy of **National Live Stock & Meat Board**

Scandinavian Burgers

1 pound lean ground beef
¾ cup shredded zucchini
⅓ cup shredded carrot
2 tablespoons finely minced onion
1 tablespoon fresh chopped dill or 1 teaspoon dried dill weed
½ teaspoon salt
Dash of freshly ground pepper
1 egg, beaten
¼ cup beer

Preheat grill.

Combine ground beef, zucchini, carrots, onions and seasonings in medium bowl; mix lightly. Stir in egg and beer. Shape into four patties.

Grill 8 minutes or to desired doneness, turning once. Serve on whole-wheat buns or rye rolls, if desired.   *Makes 4 servings*

Greek Burgers

Yogurt Sauce (recipe follows)
1 pound ground beef
2 teaspoons ground cumin
1 tablespoon chopped fresh oregano or 1 teaspoon dried leaf oregano
½ teaspoon salt
Dash of ground red pepper
Dash of black pepper
2 tablespoons red wine
Pita bread
Lettuce
Chopped tomatoes

Prepare Yogurt Sauce.

Soak 4 bamboo skewers in water. Combine meat, seasonings and wine in medium bowl; mix lightly. Divide mixture into eight equal portions; form each portion into an oval, each about 4 inches long. Cover; chill 30 minutes.

Preheat grill. Insert skewers lengthwise through centers of ovals, placing 2 on each skewer. Grill about 8 minutes or to desired doneness, turning once. Fill pita bread with lettuce, meat and chopped tomatoes. Serve with Yogurt Sauce.

Makes 4 servings

Yogurt Sauce

2 cups plain yogurt
1 cup chopped red onion
1 cup chopped cucumber
¼ cup chopped fresh mint or 1½ tablespoons dried leaf mint
1 tablespoon chopped fresh marjoram or 1 teaspoon dried leaf marjoram

Combine ingredients in small bowl. Cover; chill up to 4 hours before ready to serve.

Giant Cheeseburgers

1½ cups shredded Monterey Jack cheese (about 8 ounces)
1 can (2¼ ounces) chopped black olives
⅛ teaspoon red pepper sauce
1¾ pounds ground beef
¼ cup finely chopped onion
1 teaspoon salt
½ teaspoon black pepper
6 whole wheat hamburger buns
Butter or margarine, melted

Combine cheese, olives and red pepper sauce; mix well. Divide mixture evenly and shape into 6 balls. Mix ground beef with onion, salt and pepper; shape into 12 thin patties. Place a cheese ball in center of 6 patties and top each with a second patty. Seal edges of each patty to enclose cheese ball. Lightly oil grid. Grill patties, on covered grill, over medium-hot **KINGSFORD**® **Briquets** 5 to 6 minutes on each side or until done.

Split buns, brush with butter and place cut-sides down on grill to heat through. Serve Cheeseburgers on buns.

Nutty Burgers

1½ pounds ground beef
1 medium onion, finely chopped
1 clove garlic, finely chopped
1 cup dry bread crumbs
⅓ cup grated Parmesan cheese
⅔ cup pine nuts
⅓ cup chopped fresh parsley
2 eggs
1½ teaspoons salt
1 teaspoon pepper

Combine all ingredients; blend well. Shape into 6 thick patties. Grill patties, on covered grill, over medium-hot **KINGSFORD**® **Briquets** 5 minutes on each side or until done.

Makes 6 servings

Greek Burgers

Hot 'n' Spicy Cheeseburgers

1½ pounds ground beef
¼ cup seeded and chopped VLASIC® Hot Banana Peppers
½ teaspoon ground cumin
½ cup OPEN PIT® Original Flavor Barbecue Sauce
6 thin slices Cheddar cheese
6 onion or hamburger buns, split and toasted

1. In large bowl, combine beef, peppers and cumin. Shape into six 1-inch-thick patties.

2. On grill rack, place patties above medium coals. Grill, uncovered, until done (allow 10 minutes for medium and 12 minutes for well-done); turn and brush often with barbecue sauce. The last minute of grilling, top with cheese slices; heat until melted. Place patties on buns.

Makes 6 servings

To broil: Arrange patties on rack in broiler pan. Broil 4 inches from heat until done (allow 15 minutes for medium and 18 minutes for well-done); turn and brush often with barbecue sauce. The last minute of broiling, top with cheese slices; heat until melted.

Blue Cheese Burgers

1¼ pounds lean ground beef
1 tablespoon finely chopped onion
1½ teaspoons chopped fresh thyme or ½ teaspoon dried leaf thyme
¾ teaspoon salt
Dash of ground pepper
4 ounces blue cheese, crumbled

Preheat grill.

Combine ground beef, onions and seasonings in medium bowl; mix lightly. Shape into eight patties.

Place cheese in center of four patties to within ½ inch of outer edge; top with remaining burgers. Press edges together to seal.

Grill 8 minutes or to desired doneness, turning once. Serve with lettuce, tomatoes and Dijon-style mustard on whole-wheat buns, if desired. *Makes 4 servings*

Burgers U.S.A.

What could be more American than the humble meat patty in a bun? It's best grilled and served with relish, pickles, lettuce, tomatoes and onion.

1½ pounds ground beef
⅓ cup OPEN PIT® Original Flavor Barbecue Sauce, divided
2 tablespoons finely chopped onion
½ teaspoon dried basil leaves, crushed
½ teaspoon dried oregano leaves, crushed
6 hamburger buns, split and toasted
VLASIC® Original Hamburger Dill Chips or Hamburger Relish

1. In large bowl, combine beef, 2 tablespoons of the barbecue sauce, onion, basil and oregano. Shape into six 1-inch-thick patties.

2. On grill rack, place patties directly above medium coals. Grill, uncovered, until desired doneness (allow 10 minutes for medium and 12 minutes for well-done), turning and brushing often with remaining barbecue sauce.

3. To serve: Place patties on buns with dill chips. *Makes 6 servings*

To broil: Arrange patties on rack in broiler pan. Broil 4 inches from heat until desired doneness (allow 15 minutes for medium and 18 minutes for well-done), turning and brushing often with remaining barbecue sauce.

Swiss Burgers

1½ pounds ground beef
¾ cup shredded Swiss cheese (about 3 ounces)
1 can (8 ounces) sauerkraut, heated and drained
½ cup WISHBONE® Thousand Island or Lite Thousand Island Dressing

Shape ground beef into 6 patties. Grill or broil until done. Top evenly with cheese, sauerkraut and Thousand Island dressing. Serve, if desired, with rye or pita bread.

Makes about 6 servings

Grilled Mexican-Style Burgers

Preparation time: 10 minutes
Cooking time: 10 to 12 minutes

1 pound ground beef
2 teaspoons instant minced onion
¾ teaspoon each dried oregano leaves, ground cumin and salt
¼ teaspoon pepper
1 small tomato, cut into 8 thin slices
4 taco shells or flour tortillas
1 cup shredded lettuce
¼ cup salsa

Combine ground beef, onion, oregano, cumin, salt and pepper, mixing lightly but thoroughly. Divide beef mixture into 4 equal portions; form each into an oval shaped patty 6×2½ inches. Broil patties on grid over medium coals, turning once. Broil 10 minutes for rare; 12 minutes for medium. To assemble: arrange 2 tomato slices and a grilled burger in each taco shell. Top each with ¼ cup lettuce and 1 tablespoon salsa.

4 servings

Recipe courtesy of **National Live Stock & Meat Board.**

Bacon Burgers

1 pound lean ground beef
4 crisply cooked bacon slices, crumbled
1½ teaspoons chopped fresh thyme or ½ teaspoon dried leaf thyme
½ teaspoon salt
Dash of freshly ground pepper
4 slices Swiss cheese

Preheat grill.

Combine ground beef, bacon and seasonings in medium bowl; mix lightly. Shape into four patties.

Grill 4 minutes; turn. Top with cheese. Continue grilling 2 minutes or to desired doneness.

Makes 4 servings

Inside-Out Burgers

You'll find cheese and pickles tucked inside these grilled burgers.

1 pound ground beef
½ cup shredded sharp Cheddar cheese (2 ounces)
12 VLASIC® Bread & Butter Pickles
¼ cup OPEN PIT® Original Flavor Barbecue Sauce
4 hamburger buns, split and toasted

1. Divide beef into 8 portions; shape each portion into a ½-inch-thick patty. Place 2 tablespoons cheese and 3 pickle slices in centers of 4 patties. Top with remaining 4 patties; pinch to seal.

2. On grill rack, place filled patties directly above medium coals. Grill, uncovered, until desired doneness (allow 10 minutes for medium and 12 minutes for well-done), turning and brushing often with barbecue sauce.

3. To serve: Place patties on buns.

Makes 4 servings

To broil: Arrange patties on rack in broiler pan. Broil 4 inches from heat until desired doneness (allow 15 minutes for medium and 18 minutes for well-done), turning and brushing often with barbecue sauce.

Curried Beef Burgers

1 pound lean ground beef
¼ cup mango chutney, chopped
¼ cup grated apple
1½ teaspoons curry powder
½ teaspoon salt
Dash of freshly ground pepper
1 large red onion, sliced ¼ inch thick

Preheat grill.

Combine ground beef, chutney, apple, curry powder, salt and pepper in medium bowl; mix lightly. Shape into four patties.

Grill 8 minutes or to desired doneness, turning once. Grill onions 5 minutes or until lightly charred, turning once. Serve with burgers.

Makes 4 servings

GREAT GRILLED BURGERS

LITE & LEAN

Here's proof that a healthy diet can have lots of flavor! Each serving of these delicious lean ground beef recipes is surprisingly under 475 calories . . . a real treat for the dieter who is looking for a delicious alternative to chicken or fish.

Beef and Mushroom Filled Gougere

½ lb. extra-lean (90% lean) ground beef
½ cup chopped fresh mushrooms
1 small onion, chopped
1 garlic clove, minced
1½ teaspoons chopped fresh thyme or ½ teaspoon dried leaf thyme, crushed
  Salt and freshly ground pepper
¼ cup butter or margarine
¾ cup cold water
¾ cup all-purpose flour
½ teaspoon salt
3 eggs
¾ cup (3 ounces) shredded part-skim mozzarella cheese

Preheat oven to 425°F.

Brown ground beef in medium skillet. Drain. Add mushrooms, onions, garlic and thyme; cook until vegetables are tender. Season with salt and pepper to taste. Set aside.

Bring butter and water to boil in heavy medium saucepan. Add flour and ½ teaspoon salt, all at once. Beat with wooden spoon until mixture is smooth and forms a ball. Remove from heat. Add eggs, one at a time, beating well after each addition.

Thinly spread dough onto bottom and up sides of greased 10-inch round baking dish; fill with ground beef mixture.

Bake 25 minutes or until puffed and golden brown. Sprinkle with cheese; continue baking 5 minutes. Serve hot.   *Makes 6 servings*

Nutrient data per serving: 309 calories, 19 g fat, 166 mg cholesterol, 382 mg sodium, 23 mg iron.

Corn & Zucchini Medley

¾ lb. extra-lean (90% lean) ground beef
1 (10-ounce) package frozen whole kernel corn, thawed
2 small zucchini (approx. ½ lb.), chopped
1 large tomato, chopped
½ cup chopped onion
1 tablespoon chopped fresh basil or 1 teaspoon dried leaf basil
1½ teaspoons chopped fresh thyme or ½ teaspoon dried leaf thyme
  Salt and freshly ground pepper

Brown ground beef in large skillet. Drain. Reduce heat to medium-low. Stir in corn, zucchini, tomatoes, onions, basil and thyme; cover. Cook 10 minutes or until zucchini is tender. Season with salt and pepper to taste.   *Makes 4 servings*

Nutrient data per serving: 297 calories, 14 g fat, 71 mg cholesterol, 67 mg sodium, 3 mg iron.

Beef and Mushroom Filled Gougere

Spinach and Beef Pita Sandwiches

Perfect for a casual meal.

1 pound lean ground beef
1 package (10 ounces) frozen chopped spinach, thawed
1 bunch green onions, chopped
1 can (2¼ ounces) sliced ripe olives, drained
2 teaspoons LAWRY'S® Lemon Pepper Seasoning
1 large tomato, diced
1 cup plain non-fat yogurt or dairy sour cream
½ cup reduced-calorie mayonnaise
6 (6-inch) pita breads, warmed Lettuce leaves
1 cup (4 ounces) crumbled feta cheese

In large skillet, brown ground beef, stirring until cooked through; drain fat. Place spinach in strainer; press with back of spoon to remove as much moisture as possible. Add spinach, green onions, olives and 1 teaspoon Lemon Pepper Seasoning to beef; cook 2 minutes. Stir in tomato. In small bowl, combine yogurt, mayonnaise and remaining 1 teaspoon Lemon Pepper Seasoning. Split open pita breads. Line insides with lettuce. Stir cheese into beef mixture and divide among pita pockets. Serve with yogurt sauce.

Makes 6 servings

Presentation: Pass the remaining yogurt sauce separately.

Hint: Use scissors to cut open pita breads.

Nutrient data per serving: 439 calories, 23 g fat, 85 mg cholesterol, 678 mg sodium, 4.2 mg iron.

Warm Beef & Potato Salad

1½ lbs. russet potatoes, halved
¾ lb. extra-lean (90% lean) ground beef
1 medium garlic clove, minced
⅓ cup chicken broth
3 tablespoons tarragon-flavored vinegar or white wine vinegar
2 tablespoons olive oil
1 teaspoon sugar
3 radishes, sliced
2 green onions, chopped
1 tablespoon capers
1 tablespoon chopped fresh parsley
Salt and freshly ground pepper
Lettuce leaves
Tomato wedges (optional)

Boil potatoes, covered, in medium saucepan 25 minutes or until tender. (Do not overcook.)

Meanwhile, brown ground beef in medium skillet. Drain. Add garlic; cook until tender.

Drain potatoes; cool slightly. Slice potatoes; place in medium bowl. Whisk together broth, vinegar, oil and sugar in small bowl. Pour over warm potatoes; toss lightly.

Add ground beef mixture, radishes, onions, capers and parsley; mix carefully to avoid breaking up potatoes. Season with salt and pepper to taste.

Serve on lettuce-covered plates. Garnish with tomato wedges, if desired.

Makes 4 servings

Nutrient data per serving: 434 calories, 21 g fat, 711 mg cholesterol, 143 mg sodium, 2.7 mg iron.

Spinach and Beef Pita Sandwiches

Thai Beef Salad with Cucumber Dressing

Cool cooked ramen noodles in a bowl of iced water; drain well just before serving.

Cucumber Dressing (recipe follows)
1 lb. extra-lean (90% lean) ground beef
½ red pepper, cut in thin strips
6 mushrooms, quartered
2 green onions, diagonally cut into 1-inch pieces
1 garlic clove, minced
1 tablespoon seasoned rice vinegar
1 teaspoon soy sauce
Salt and freshly ground pepper
Lettuce leaves
3 ounces ramen noodles, cooked
12 cherry tomatoes, halved
Mint sprigs

Prepare Cucumber Dressing; set aside.

Brown ground beef in medium skillet. Drain. Add red peppers, mushrooms, onions and garlic; cook until tender. Stir in vinegar and soy sauce; season with salt and pepper to taste.

Arrange lettuce leaves on four luncheon-size plates. Top with noodles and ground beef mixture. Garnish with cherry tomatoes and mint sprigs. Serve with dressing.

Makes 4 servings

Cucumber Dressing

1 medium cucumber, coarsely chopped
½ cup coarsely chopped onion
½ cup loosely packed cilantro leaves
1 garlic clove, minced
1 tablespoon diced jalapeño or green chili pepper
½ cup seasoned rice vinegar

Place cucumbers, onions, cilantro, garlic and peppers in food processor container; process 1 minute. Spoon mixture into small bowl; stir in vinegar.

Nutrient data per serving: 367 calories, 21 g fat, 98 mg cholesterol, 313 mg sodium, 4.3 mg iron.

Spinach-Potato Bake

1 lb. extra-lean (90% lean) ground beef
½ cup fresh mushroom slices
1 small onion, chopped
2 garlic cloves, minced
1 (10-ounce) package frozen chopped spinach, thawed, well drained
½ teaspoon grated nutmeg
1 lb. russet potatoes, peeled, cooked, mashed
¼ cup light sour cream
¼ cup skim milk
Salt and freshly ground pepper
½ cup (2 ounces) shredded Cheddar cheese

Preheat oven to 400°F. Spray deep 9-inch casserole dish with nonstick cooking spray.

Brown ground beef in large skillet. Drain. Add mushrooms, onions and garlic; cook until tender. Stir in spinach and nutmeg; cover. Heat thoroughly, stirring occasionally.

Combine potatoes, sour cream and milk. Add to ground beef mixture; season with salt and pepper to taste. Spoon into prepared casserole dish; sprinkle with cheese.

Bake 15 to 20 minutes or until slightly puffed and cheese is melted.

Makes 6 servings

Nutrient data per serving: 341 calories, 17 g fat, 77 mg cholesterol, 166 mg sodium, 3.1 mg iron.

Thai Beef Salad with Cucumber Dressing

Stuffed Mushrooms with Tomato Sauce and Pasta

Tomato Sauce (recipe follows)
1 lb. extra-lean (90% lean) ground beef
¼ cup finely chopped onion
¼ cup finely chopped green or red pepper
1 large garlic clove, minced
2 tablespoons finely chopped parsley
2 teaspoons finely chopped fresh basil or 1 teaspoon dried leaf basil, crushed
1 teaspoon finely chopped fresh oregano or ½ teaspoon dried leaf oregano, crushed
½ teaspoon salt
Dash of freshly ground pepper
12 very large mushrooms
¼ cup (1 ounce) grated Parmesan cheese
4½ cups cooked spaghetti

Prepare Tomato Sauce; set aside.

Preheat oven to 350°F.

Combine ground beef, onions, green peppers, garlic, parsley, basil, oregano, salt and pepper in medium bowl; mix lightly. Remove stems from mushrooms; finely chop stems. Add to ground beef mixture. Stuff into mushroom caps, rounding tops.

Pour Tomato Sauce into shallow casserole dish large enough to hold mushrooms in single layer. Place mushrooms, stuffing side up, in sauce; cover.

Bake 20 minutes; remove cover. Sprinkle with Parmesan cheese. Continue baking, uncovered, 15 minutes. Serve with spaghetti. Garnish with additional fresh basil leaves, if desired.

Makes 6 servings

Tomato Sauce

2 (14½-ounce) cans tomatoes, chopped, undrained
Dash of hot pepper sauce
1 teaspoon finely chopped fresh marjoram or ½ teaspoon dried leaf marjoram, crushed
1 teaspoon fennel seeds, crushed
Salt and freshly ground pepper

Combine all ingredients except salt and pepper in medium saucepan. Bring to boil. Reduce heat; simmer 5 minutes. Season with salt and pepper to taste.

Nutrient data per serving: 409 calories, 15 g fat, 664 mg cholesterol, 556 mg sodium, 4.8 mg iron.

Roasted Bell Pepper Quesadillas

½ lb. extra-lean (90% lean) ground beef
¼ cup chopped onion
Salt and freshly ground black pepper
1 cup (4 ounces) shredded provolone cheese
8 (6-inch) extra-thin corn tortillas
½ cup roasted bell pepper strips
¼ cup chopped cilantro

Brown ground beef in medium skillet. Drain. Add onions; cook until tender. Season with salt and pepper to taste.

Sprinkle 2 tablespoons cheese onto each of four tortillas; cover with ground beef mixture, pepper strips, cilantro and remaining cheese. Top with remaining tortillas.

Cook, in batches, in nonstick skillet over medium heat about 4 minutes or until cheese is melted, carefully turning after 2 minutes.

Makes 4 servings

Nutrient data per serving: 387 calories, 19.3 g fat, 68 mg cholesterol, 339 mg sodium, 3 mg iron.

Stuffed Mushrooms with Tomato Sauce and Pasta

Beef with Snow Peas & Baby Corn

¾ lb. extra-lean (90% lean) ground beef
1 garlic clove, minced
1 teaspoon vegetable oil
6 ounces snow peas, halved lengthwise
1 red pepper, cut into strips
1 (15-ounce) can baby corn, drained, rinsed
1 tablespoon soy sauce
1 teaspoon sesame oil
Salt and freshly ground pepper
2 cups cooked rice

Brown ground beef in wok or large skillet. Drain. Add garlic; cook until tender. Set aside. Wipe out wok with paper towel.

Heat vegetable oil in wok over medium-high heat. Add snow peas and red peppers; stir-fry 2 to 3 minutes or until vegetables are crisp-tender. Stir in ground beef mixture, baby corn, soy sauce and sesame oil. Season with salt and pepper to taste. Serve over rice.

Makes 4 servings

Nutrient data per serving: 461 calories, 17 g fat, 71 mg cholesterol, 625 mg sodium, 5 mg iron.

Greek Pasta Salad

½ lb. extra-lean (90% lean) ground beef
⅓ cup chopped fresh mint or 2 tablespoons dried leaf mint
1 garlic clove, minced
1¾ cups (approx. 6 ounces) small shell macaroni, cooked
10 cherry tomatoes, quartered
2 ounces feta cheese, crumbled
½ red pepper, chopped
½ red onion, cut into rings
¼ cup reduced-calorie Italian dressing
2 tablespoons lemon juice
Salt and freshly ground black pepper
Lettuce leaves

Brown ground beef in medium skillet. Drain. Add mint and garlic; cook 2 minutes, stirring constantly.

Spoon ground beef mixture into large bowl. Stir in pasta, tomatoes, cheese, red peppers and onions. Add dressing and lemon juice; toss lightly. Season with salt and pepper to taste. Serve on lettuce-covered salad plates. *Makes 4 servings*

Note: Salad can be made up to 4 hours in advance.

Nutrient data per serving: 342 calories, 15 g fat, 892 mg cholesterol, 330 mg sodium, 3.2 mg iron.

Beef Fried Rice

¾ lb. extra-lean (90% lean) ground beef
6 green onions, chopped
3 large celery stalks, chopped
8 ounces bean sprouts
½ cup chopped fresh mushrooms
½ cup finely chopped red pepper
1 teaspoon grated gingerroot
3 cups cooked rice
2 tablespoons soy sauce
Salt and freshly ground black pepper

Brown ground beef in large skillet. Drain. Stir in onions, celery, bean sprouts, mushrooms, red peppers and gingerroot. Cook over medium-high heat 5 minutes or until vegetables are crisp-tender, stirring frequently. Stir in rice and soy sauce. Season with salt and black pepper to taste. Heat thoroughly, stirring occasionally. *Makes 4 servings*

Variation: Substitute low-sodium soy sauce for soy sauce.

Nutrient data per serving: 425 calories, 14 g fat, 71 mg cholesterol, 609 mg sodium, 4.9 mg iron.

Beef with Snow Peas & Baby Corn

Asparagus-Mushroom Stir-Fry

¾ pound extra-lean (90% lean) ground beef
4 green onions, chopped
1 garlic clove, minced
2 teaspoons grated fresh gingerroot
1 teaspoon vegetable oil
1 pound asparagus spears, diagonally cut into 1-inch pieces
1 cup quartered fresh mushrooms
1 tablespoon soy sauce
  Salt and freshly ground pepper
4 ounces ramen noodles, cooked, drained

Brown ground beef in wok or large skillet. Drain. Add onions, garlic and gingerroot; cook 1 minute. Set aside.

Wipe out wok with paper towel. Add oil to wok; heat over medium-high heat. Add asparagus and mushrooms; stir-fry 2 or 3 minutes or until asparagus is crisp-tender.

Add ground beef mixture to vegetables in wok; stir until heated thoroughly. Stir in soy sauce; season with salt and pepper to taste. Add noodles; toss lightly.

Makes 4 servings

Nutrient data per serving: 294 calories, 17 g fat, 71 mg cholesterol, 426 mg sodium, 3.3 mg iron.

Cantaloupe & Beef Salad

1 lb. extra-lean (90% lean) ground beef
3 tablespoons chopped fresh mint or 1 tablespoon dried leaf mint
1 garlic clove, minced
  Salt and freshly ground pepper
4 cups cantaloupe balls
1 cup cubed jicama
½ cup creamy reduced-calorie Italian dressing
8 cups torn lettuce leaves

Brown ground beef in medium skillet. Drain. Add mint and garlic; cook 2 minutes, stirring constantly. Season with salt and pepper to taste.

Combine ground beef mixture, cantaloupe and jicama in serving bowl; stir in dressing. Add lettuce; toss lightly.   *Makes 4 servings*

Nutrient data per serving: 402 calories, 22 g fat, 97 mg cholesterol, 345 mg sodium, 4.8 mg iron.

Taco Salad

1 lb. extra-lean (90% lean) ground beef
1 small onion, finely chopped
1 garlic clove, minced
2 teaspoons chili powder
1 teaspoon ground cumin
½ teaspoon salt
  Dash of freshly ground black pepper
1 large head iceberg lettuce, torn into bite-size pieces (approx. 10 cups)
2 large tomatoes
1 medium avocado, peeled, sliced
2 cups salsa

Brown ground beef in medium skillet. Drain. Add onions and garlic; cook until tender. Stir in seasonings.

Combine lettuce, tomatoes and avocado in large serving bowl; toss lightly. Top with ground beef mixture. Serve with salsa.

Makes 4 servings

Nutrient data per serving: 453 calories, 30 g fat, 95 mg cholesterol, 826 mg sodium, 5.9 mg iron.

Artichoke Casserole

¾ lb. extra-lean (90% lean)
    ground beef
½ cup fresh mushroom slices
¼ cup chopped onion
1 garlic clove, minced
1 (14-ounce) can artichoke hearts,
    drained, rinsed, chopped
½ cup dry bread crumbs
¼ cup (1 ounce) grated Parmesan
    cheese
2 tablespoons chopped fresh
    rosemary or 1 teaspoon dried
    leaf rosemary
1½ teaspoons chopped fresh
    marjoram or ½ teaspoon dried
    leaf marjoram
  Salt and freshly ground pepper
3 egg whites

Preheat oven to 400°F. Spray 1-quart
casserole with nonstick cooking spray.

Brown ground beef in medium skillet.
Drain. Add mushrooms, onions and
garlic; cook until tender.

Combine ground beef, artichokes,
crumbs, cheese, rosemary and
marjoram; mix lightly. Season with
salt and pepper to taste.

Beat egg whites until stiff peaks form;
fold into ground beef mixture. Spoon
into prepared casserole.

Bake 20 minutes or until lightly
browned around edges.

Makes 4 servings

Nutrient data per serving: 364 calories,
17 g fat, 76 mg cholesterol, 375 mg
sodium, 4.4 mg iron.

Calzones

½ lb. extra-lean (90% lean)
    ground beef
2 green peppers, thinly sliced
½ cup fresh mushroom slices
1 medium onion, thinly sliced
1 garlic clove, minced
1 tablespoon chopped fresh
    oregano or 1 teaspoon dried
    leaf oregano
1 tablespoon chopped fresh basil
    or 2 teaspoons dried leaf basil
  Dash of hot pepper flakes
    (optional)
  Salt and freshly ground black
    pepper
1 loaf frozen whole-wheat bread
    dough, thawed
4 ounces feta cheese, crumbled
⅓ cup (1½ ounces) grated
    Parmesan cheese

Brown ground beef in medium skillet.
Drain. Add peppers, mushrooms,
onions and garlic; cook until
vegetables are tender and all liquid
has evaporated. Stir in oregano,
basil and pepper flakes; season with
salt and pepper to taste. Set aside.

Preheat oven to 400°F.

Divide dough into six equal pieces.
For each calzone, roll out one piece
of dough on lightly floured surface to
8-inch circle. Spoon ground beef
mixture onto center of dough; top
with cheeses. Lightly dampen edges
of dough with water. Bring edges
together over filling; press edges
together with fork to seal. Place on
nonstick baking sheet.

Bake 15 minutes or until golden
brown. *Makes 6 servings*

Nutrient data per serving: 360 calories,
14 g fat, 53 mg cholesterol, 730 mg
sodium, 3.4 mg iron.

With today's active lifestyles, home-cooked meals are often only a weekend luxury. Rediscover the pleasures of cooking any day of the week with these fabulous recipes designed just for the microwave . . . and you! In minutes, you'll have a satisfying dinner on the table with a minimum of time and effort.

Easy Pepper Steak

1 pound lean ground beef
1 tablespoon chopped fresh
thyme or 1 teaspoon dried
leaf thyme
1 teaspoon paprika
Salt and freshly ground black
pepper
3 tablespoons all-purpose flour
1¼ cups chicken broth
2 tablespoons dry white wine
1 teaspoon Worcestershire sauce
3 medium bell peppers
(use 1 each red, green and
yellow, if possible), cut into
thin slices
1 medium onion, sliced,
separated into rings

Crumble ground beef into large bowl. Stir in thyme, paprika, 1 teaspoon salt and dash of black pepper. Shape into four ½-inch-thick oval loaves. Place on microwave-safe rack; cover with waxed paper. Microwave on HIGH 4 to 5 minutes or to desired doneness, turning rack after 3 minutes. Reserve ⅓ cup meat drippings; keep meat warm. Mix together drippings and flour in a medium microwave-safe bowl. Stir in broth, wine and Worcestershire sauce. Microwave on HIGH 2 to 3 minutes or until mixture thickens, stirring every minute. Season with salt and pepper to taste. Add bell peppers and onions; cover. Microwave on HIGH 6 to 7 minutes or until vegetables are crisp-tender, stirring after 3 minutes. Serve over meat. *Makes 4 servings*

Lipton Onion Burgers

1 envelope LIPTON® Onion Recipe
Soup Mix
2 pounds ground beef
½ cup water

In large bowl, combine all ingredients; shape into 8 patties. Place 4 patties in microwave-safe oblong baking dish and microwave uncovered at HIGH (Full Power) 6 minutes, turning patties once. Repeat with remaining patties. Let stand covered 5 minutes. Serve, if desired, with toasted hamburger buns. *Makes 8 servings*

Tempting Taco Burgers: Add 2 teaspoons chili powder to ground beef mixture. Microwave as above. Top with shredded lettuce, Cheddar cheese and chopped tomatoes.

Conventional Directions: Prepare patties as above. Grill or broil until done. Serve as above.

Also terrific with LIPTON® Beefy Onion or Beefy Mushroom Recipe Soup Mix.

Easy Pepper Steak

Spicy Beef-Topped Potatoes

Preparation time: 5 minutes
Cooking time: 15 to 18 minutes

1 pound ground beef (80% lean)
2 large baking potatoes
½ cup chopped onion
1 jar (12 ounces) picante sauce
½ teaspoon salt
2 slices (1 ounce each) Cheddar cheese, cut diagonally into quarters*
1 green onion, sliced

Scrub potatoes; prick each with fork in several places. Microwave at HIGH 8 to 10 minutes or until tender, rotating ¼ turn after 4 minutes. Let stand while preparing topping. Combine ground beef and chopped onion; arrange in a ring in microwave-safe sieve or colander. Place sieve in microwave-safe bowl; microwave at HIGH 3 minutes. Stir to break up beef. Continue cooking at HIGH 3 minutes; stir. Pour off drippings. Place beef in same bowl. Add picante sauce, stirring to combine. Microwave at HIGH 1 to 2 minutes or until heated through. Cut potatoes in half lengthwise; break up and fluff pulp with fork. Sprinkle with salt. Spoon an equal amount of beef mixture over each potato half. Top each with an equal amount of cheese; tent loosely with foil and let stand 1 minute. Garnish with sliced green onion.

Makes 4 servings

*Mozzarella or brick cheese slices may be substituted for the cheddar cheese.

Recipe courtesy of **National Live Stock & Meat Board**

Special San Francisco Pita Pocket

A great sandwich for lunch or brunch.

1 package (10 ounces) frozen chopped spinach
¾ pound lean ground beef
½ pound fresh mushrooms, sliced
½ cup chopped onion
3 tablespoons butter or margarine
¾ teaspoon dill weed
½ teaspoon LAWRY'S® Seasoned Salt
½ teaspoon LAWRY'S® Garlic Powder with Parsley
½ teaspoon LAWRY'S® Seasoned Pepper
2 cups (8 ounces) grated cheese (½ Cheddar and ½ Monterey Jack)
4 pita breads, cut in half

Make slit in spinach package; place package, slit side up, on paper towel. Microwave on HIGH 5 minutes. Remove spinach from package; squeeze liquid from spinach. In microwave-safe pie plate or dish, microwave ground beef on HIGH 6 to 7 minutes, stirring once or twice. Drain fat. In 13 x 9 x 2-inch microwave-safe baking dish, microwave mushrooms, onion and butter on HIGH 8 to 10 minutes. Stir in seasonings. Microwave on HIGH 3 minutes, stirring once. Stir spinach and cooked ground beef into mushroom-onion mixture. Fold in cheese. Cover with waxed paper and microwave on High 3 minutes. Wrap pita breads loosely in plastic wrap; microwave on HIGH 30 seconds to warm. Open pita breads and fill with meat mixture. Serve immediately.

Makes 8 servings

Presentation: Serve with assorted fresh fruit.

Spicy Beef-Topped Potatoes

Zesty Zucchini Lasagna

1 package (1.5 ounces) LAWRY'S® Spaghetti Sauce Seasoning Blend with Imported Mushrooms
1 can (6 ounces) tomato paste
1¾ cups water
2 tablespoons IMPERIAL® Margarine
1 pound ground beef
½ teaspoon basil leaves
⅛ teaspoon thyme leaves
2 cups ricotta cheese
1 egg, slightly beaten
4 medium zucchini, thinly sliced lengthwise
1 cup shredded mozzarella cheese (about 4 ounces)

In 1-quart glass measure, combine Spaghetti Sauce Seasoning Blend with Imported Mushrooms, tomato paste, water and margarine. Cover with wax paper and microwave at HIGH (Full Power) 15 minutes, stirring every 4 minutes. In 1-quart microwave-safe casserole, place ground beef. Microwave at HIGH 5 minutes or until no longer pink, stirring once. Drain fat; crumble beef. Stir in prepared spaghetti sauce, basil and thyme; set aside. In small bowl, combine ricotta cheese with egg. In 12 x 8-inch microwave-safe casserole, arrange zucchini; sprinkle with water. Cover with plastic wrap, venting one corner, and microwave at HIGH 2 minutes; drain liquid. In same dish, layer ½ of the zucchini, ricotta mixture and meat sauce. Repeat layers. Cover with plastic wrap, venting one corner, and microwave at HIGH 14 minutes, turning casserole once. Sprinkle with mozzarella cheese; microwave uncovered at HIGH 3 minutes or until cheese is melted.   *Makes about 6 servings*

Beef and Mushroom Ring

¾ cup water
2 tablespoons butter or margarine
2 cups herb-seasoned dry stuffing mix
1½ pounds ground beef
2 large eggs
⅓ cup finely chopped onion
¼ cup unseasoned fine dry bread crumbs
1 tablespoon catsup
1 tablespoon minced fresh parsley
1 teaspoon Worcestershire sauce
1 teaspoon salt
½ teaspoon dried thyme, crumbled
¼ teaspoon pepper
2 cans (4 ounces each) sliced mushrooms, drained
1 medium onion
Parsley sprigs, if desired

1. Place water and butter in medium microwave-safe bowl. Microwave, uncovered, at High until boiling, 1½ to 2 minutes. Add stuffing mix; mix well.

2. Combine beef, eggs, chopped onion, bread crumbs, catsup, minced parsley, Worcestershire sauce, salt, thyme and pepper in second medium bowl; mix well.

3. Spread 1 can of the mushrooms in even layer in bottom of 6-cup microwave-safe ring mold. Cut medium onion crosswise into ⅛-inch-thick slices; separate slices into rings. Arrange onion rings in even layer over mushrooms.

4. Spread ⅓ of the meat mixture evenly over onion rings in mold. Add the remaining can of mushrooms to stuffing mixture; mix well. Spoon ½ of the stuffing mixture in a ring in center of meat layer, leaving 1-inch borders around outer edge and center of mold.

5. Top stuffing layer with ⅓ of the meat mixture; spread evenly. Press inner and outer edges firmly with fingers to seal. Make a second layer of stuffing as in Step 4. Top with remaining ⅓ meat mixture and seal edges.

6. Microwave meatloaf ring, covered with waxed paper, at High power until meat is firm and no longer pink, 8 to 10 minutes; rotate mold ½ turn after about half of cooking time. Let meatloaf ring stand, covered tightly with aluminum foil, 10 minutes.

7. Drain off any liquid that collects around sides of mold. Unmold meatloaf ring onto serving dish. Garnish with parsley sprigs. Cut into thick slices or wedges to serve.

Makes 6 servings

Souperior Meat Loaf

1 envelope LIPTON® Onion Recipe Soup Mix
2 pounds ground beef
1½ cups fresh bread crumbs
2 eggs
¾ cup water
⅓ cup ketchup

In large bowl, combine all ingredients. In 2-quart microwave-safe oblong baking dish, shape into loaf. Microwave uncovered at HIGH (Full Power), turning dish occasionally, 25 minutes or until done; drain. Let stand covered 5 minutes.

Makes about 8 servings

Conventional Directions: Preheat oven to 350°. Combine as above. In large baking pan, shape into loaf. Bake 1 hour or until done.

Also terrific with LIPTON® Beefy Onion, Onion-Mushroom or Beefy Mushroom Recipe Soup Mix.

Meatballs Oriental

2 cans (8 ounces each) pineapple chunks in natural juice, undrained
¼ cup cornstarch
1 cup chicken broth
½ cup packed brown sugar
½ cup cider vinegar
2 tablespoons rice wine or dry sherry
5 tablespoons soy sauce
½ pound ground beef
½ pound lean ground pork
1 large egg, lightly beaten
¼ cup fine dry bread crumbs
2 tablespoons minced green onion
1 teaspoon minced fresh gingerroot
⅛ teaspoon black pepper
1 large green bell pepper, cut into thin strips
3 cups hot cooked rice

1. Drain pineapple, reserving ½ cup of the juice. Mix together cornstarch and the reserved juice in 2-quart microwave-safe casserole until smooth. Add broth, sugar, vinegar, rice wine and 3 tablespoons of the soy sauce; stir until sugar dissolves.

2. Microwave sauce mixture, uncovered, at High power until thick and shiny, 7 to 9 minutes; stir with whisk twice during cooking. Reserve sauce.

3. While sauce is cooking, combine beef, pork, egg, bread crumbs, onion, gingerroot, black pepper and remaining 2 tablespoons soy sauce in medium bowl; mix well. Shape into 20 meatballs 1 to 1½ inches in diameter. Place balls in 12 x 8-inch baking dish.

4. Scatter green pepper over meatballs. Microwave, uncovered, at High power until meatballs are cooked through and no longer pink inside, 6 to 8 minutes; stir mixture to rearrange once during cooking.

5. Drain fat from meatballs. Add meatballs, green peppers and pineapple to reserved sauce; stir to mix well. Microwave, uncovered, at High power until hot, 4 to 6 minutes; stir once during heating. Serve over hot cooked rice.

Makes 4 servings

Beef & Broccoli

1 pound lean ground beef
4 tablespoons soy sauce, divided
2 tablespoons dry sherry
1 tablespoon all-purpose flour
1 tablespoon sugar
1 tablespoon seasoned rice vinegar
2 teaspoons grated gingerroot or 1 teaspoon ground ginger
1 pound fresh broccoli, stems sliced, tops broken in flowerets (about 6 cups)
1 medium onion, sliced crosswise, separated into rings
  Dash of hot pepper sauce
  Salt and freshly ground pepper
  Hot cooked rice

Crumble ground beef into large microwave-safe bowl. Stir together soy sauce, sherry, flour, sugar, vinegar and gingerroot in 2-cup glass measure. Add to ground beef; mix well. Cover; chill 30 minutes.

Microwave marinated ground beef mixture, uncovered, on HIGH 6 minutes or until ground beef is no longer pink, stirring twice during cooking. Drain; keep meat warm.

Combine broccoli and onions in microwave-safe casserole dish. Cover with plastic wrap; vent. Microwave on HIGH 5 to 6 minutes or until crisp-tender. Add to meat with hot pepper sauce; mix lightly. Season with salt and pepper to taste. Serve with rice.

Makes 4 servings

Variation: Stir in 1 medium tomato, chopped, just before serving.

Recipe courtesy of **Rice Council**

Festive Chili con Carne

1 pound ground beef or pork
1 medium onion, chopped
1 medium green bell pepper, chopped
1 clove garlic, minced
2 to 4 teaspoons chili powder
1 teaspoon salt
½ teaspoon dried oregano, crumbled
1 can (16 ounces) whole tomatoes, undrained
1 can (8 ounces) tomato sauce
1 can (15 ounces) red kidney beans, drained
1 tablespoon red wine vinegar
  Tortilla chips or crackers

1. Crumble meat into microwave-safe plastic colander.* Place colander in 2-quart microwave-safe casserole. Microwave, uncovered, at High power until meat is no longer pink, 4 to 6 minutes; stir with fork to break up meat every 2 minutes during cooking.

2. Discard meat drippings from casserole. Transfer meat from colander to casserole; break up into small pieces with back of spoon. Stir in onion, green pepper and garlic. Microwave, uncovered, at High power until onion and pepper are tender, 4 to 5 minutes.

3. Add chili powder, salt and oregano to casserole; mix well. Drain tomato liquid into casserole. Chop tomatoes in can with scissors or knife; add to casserole. Add tomato sauce and beans; mix well. Microwave, covered with lid, at High power 5 minutes.

4. Add vinegar to chili; stir to mix well. Microwave, uncovered, at Medium (50%) power 20 to 25 minutes until slightly thickened and to allow flavors to blend; stir twice during cooking. Serve with chips or crackers.

Makes 4 servings

*For microwave-safe colander, use dishwasher-safe plastic colander with no metal parts.

Beef & Broccoli

Quick and Easy Tamale Pie

½ pound ground beef
¼ cup sliced green onions
2 envelopes LIPTON® Tomato Cup-a-Soup Instant Soup
¼ cup water
1 can (7 ounces) whole kernel corn, drained
2 tablespoons chopped pitted ripe olives (optional)
¼ teaspoon chili powder
3 slices (¾ ounce each) American cheese, halved
2 corn muffins, cut into ½-inch cubes
Mexican Sour Cream Topping (optional)

In shallow microwave-safe 1-quart casserole, microwave ground beef with green onions at HIGH (Full Power) 2½ minutes or until beef is no longer pink, stirring once. Stir in instant tomato soup mix, water, corn, olives and chili powder until well blended. Top with cheese, then evenly spread muffin cubes over cheese. Microwave at HIGH 5 minutes or until heated through and cheese is melted, turning casserole once. Garnish, if desired, with fresh coriander (cilantro), sliced pitted ripe olives and jalapeño peppers. Serve with Mexican Sour Cream Topping if desired.

Makes 2 main-dish or 4 snack-size servings

Mexican Sour Cream Topping:
Blend ½ cup sour cream, 2 tablespoons chopped jalapeño peppers and 1 teaspoon lime juice.

Note: Recipe can be doubled. Prepare in a 2-quart microwave-safe shallow casserole and microwave ground beef 6 minutes or until no longer pink, stirring twice. Increase the final cooking time to 8 minutes or until heated through and cheese is melted.

Conventional Directions: Increase water to ½ cup. In medium skillet, brown ground beef. Stir in instant tomato soup mix, water, corn, green onions, olives and chili powder until well blended. Top with cheese and muffin cubes as above. Cook 5 minutes or until heated through and cheese is melted. Garnish as above.

Baked Beef and Rice Marinara

1 pound lean ground beef
¾ cup sliced fresh mushrooms
½ cup EACH chopped onions, chopped celery and diced green pepper
2 cups cooked rice
¾ teaspoon ground oregano
½ teaspoon EACH salt, basil and garlic powder
1 can (15 ounces) tomato sauce
3 slices American cheese

Combine crumbled beef and vegetables in plastic colander; place colander over 2-quart microwave-safe baking dish. Cook, uncovered, on HIGH (maximum power) 4 minutes; stir after 2 minutes. Drain beef; return mixture to baking dish. Stir in remaining ingredients except cheese. Cook on HIGH 2 minutes. Arrange cheese slices on top; cook on HIGH 2 minutes. Let stand 5 minutes.

Makes 4 servings

Conventional Directions: Cook beef and vegetables over medium-high heat in large skillet until meat is no longer pink and vegetables are crisp-tender, stirring frequently. Combine meat mixture with remaining ingredients except cheese in buttered 2-quart baking dish; arrange cheese slices on top. Bake at 350 degrees 20 to 25 minutes.

Recipe courtesy of **Rice Council**

Beefy Cabbage Rolls

1 head green cabbage
1½ cups sliced fresh mushrooms
1 can (16 ounces) tomatoes,
    drained and chopped
2 cups shredded cooked beef
1 cup shredded carrots
⅔ cup chopped onion
1 teaspoon dried basil
1 clove garlic, minced
½ teaspoon salt
¼ teaspoon dried rosemary
¼ teaspoon grated lemon rind
⅛ teaspoon pepper
2 tablespoons olive oil
1 can (15 ounces) tomato sauce
2 tablespoons packed brown
    sugar
1 tablespoon cider vinegar
1 teaspoon instant beef bouillon
    granules

1. Cut center core from cabbage; discard. Wrap cabbage in plastic wrap; microwave at High power just until outer leaves can be separated from head, 1½ to 3½ minutes.

2. Remove 8 cabbage leaves; cut out hard center rib at base of each leaf. Spread leaves on microwave-safe baking sheet. Microwave, covered with plastic wrap, at High power until pliable, 1 to 2½ minutes. Reserve.

3. Shred enough of the remaining cabbage to make 1½ cups. (Refrigerate remaining cabbage, wrapped in plastic, for other use.) Combine shredded cabbage and mushrooms in 2-quart microwave-safe casserole. Microwave, covered with lid, at HIGH power until cabbage is tender, 3 to 6 minutes; stir twice during cooking. Drain well.

4. Add tomatoes, beef, carrot, ⅓ cup onion, ½ teaspoon basil, the garlic, salt, rosemary, lemon rind and pepper to mushroom mixture; mix well.

5. Spoon ⅛ of the beef filling onto center of each cabbage leaf. Fold sides of each leaf over filling; roll up securely and fasten at seam with wooden pick. Place rolls seam-side-down in 12 × 8-inch baking dish.

6. For sauce, combine remaining ⅓ cup onion and the oil in medium microwave-safe bowl. Microwave, uncovered, at HIGH power until onion is tender, 2 to 3 minutes. Stir in the remaining ½ teaspoon basil and the remaining ingredients. Microwave, uncovered, at HIGH power until sauce is thickened, 8 to 12 minutes; stir 2 to 3 times during cooking.

7. Remove wooden picks from cabbage rolls. Pour sauce over cabbage rolls. Microwave, covered with plastic wrap, at High power until heated through, 6 to 10 minutes; rotate dish ½ turn twice during cooking. Let stand 5 minutes before serving.

Makes 4 servings

Sloppy Joes

1 pound ground beef
2 envelopes LIPTON® Onion
    Cup-a-Soup Instant Soup
1 can (8 ounces) tomato sauce
2 teaspoons sugar
½ teaspoon prepared mustard

In 1½-quart microwave-safe casserole, microwave ground beef, uncovered, at HIGH (Full Power) 3 minutes or until no longer pink, stirring once; drain. Stir in remaining ingredients and microwave at HIGH 4 minutes, stirring once. Serve on toasted hamburger rolls.

Makes about 4 servings

Conventional Directions: In medium skillet, brown ground beef; drain. Stir in remaining ingredients and simmer 5 minutes or until heated through. Serve as above.

Beefy Cabbage Rolls

LET'S PARTY!

Menu planning can be the most challenging part of entertaining. Now it's easy with these fantastic menus geared for year-round festivities. Whether you're in search of an elegant New Year's brunch menu or fun foods for a children's Halloween party, you'll find complete menu ideas right here. Some menus even offer you several recipe selections to choose from. So plan your next celebration with confidence . . . and enjoy the party!

Winter Ambrosia with Coconut Dressing

1 large grapefruit
2 large oranges
1 banana
½ cup shredded coconut
   Coconut Dressing (recipe follows)
¼ cup pecan pieces, toasted

Section grapefruit and oranges, reserving juice for Coconut Dressing. Slice banana into ½-inch pieces; dip into reserved juice. Combine grapefruit, oranges, banana and coconut in serving bowl; toss lightly. Cover; chill.

Prepare Coconut Dressing; cool.

Stir dressing into fruit mixture just before serving. Add pecans; mix lightly. Garnish with mint leaf, if desired.

Coconut Dressing

Reserved grapefruit and orange juices
1 tablespoon sugar
1 (5.6-fluid-ounce) can coconut milk (2/3 cup)
2 teaspoons cornstarch

Pour reserved grapefruit and orange juices into medium saucepan. Bring to boil. Reduce heat to medium; simmer until juice is reduced by half. Stir in sugar. Stir small amount of coconut milk into cornstarch. Add with remaining coconut milk to juice in saucepan. Cook until bubbly and thickened, stirring constantly. Cool.

Makes 6 servings

Spinach Salad with Creamy Tarragon Dressing

1 bunch fresh spinach
2 cups torn lettuce
1 small head cauliflower, thinly sliced
½ cup sour cream
½ cup mayonnaise
2 teaspoons Dijon-style mustard
¾ teaspoon chopped fresh tarragon or ¼ teaspoon dried leaf tarragon
Salt and freshly ground pepper
Crisply fried bacon slices, chopped
Shredded Cheddar cheese
Crumbled blue cheese
Croutons
Chopped green onions
Sunflower kernels

Wash spinach well. Remove large stems; tear large leaves into smaller pieces. Combine with lettuce and cauliflower in large bowl; cover. Chill.

Combine sour cream, mayonnaise, mustard and tarragon in small bowl. Season with salt and pepper to taste. (Note: Mixture may be thinned with a little milk, if desired.) Cover; chill.

When ready to serve, surround bowl of spinach mixture with smaller bowls of bacon, cheeses, croutons, green onions and sunflower kernels. Serve with sour cream mixture.

Makes about 6 servings

Clockwise from top: Cherry Streusel Coffeecake (page 77), Beef & Cabbage Puff (page 77), Winter Ambrosia with Coconut Dressing and Creamy Coffee (page 76).

Black-Eyed Pea Salad

½ lb. lean ground beef
2 (15-ounce) cans black-eyed
  peas, drained, rinsed
1 red pepper, chopped
1 cup celery slices
¼ cup chopped fresh parsley
2 tablespoons seasoned rice
  vinegar
1 tablespoon balsamic vinegar or
  wine vinegar
2 tablespoons olive oil
  Salt and freshly ground black
  pepper

Brown ground beef in medium skillet. Drain.

Combine ground beef, peas, red pepper, celery and parsley in medium bowl. Whisk together vinegars and oil in small bowl. Add to ground beef mixture; toss lightly. Season with salt and pepper to taste; cover. Chill several hours or overnight, stirring occasionally. Serve in spinach-lined bowl and garnish with cherry tomato halves, if desired.
Makes 6 servings

Variation: Substitute 3½ cups cooked fresh black-eyed peas or 15-ounce can red kidney beans, drained, for canned peas.

Creamy Coffee

6 cups strong coffee
3 cups vanilla ice cream
2 tablespoons vanilla extract
1 strip orange peel
1 cup whipping cream, whipped
  Ground cinnamon

Combine coffee, ice cream, vanilla and orange peel in large saucepan. Stir over low heat until ice cream is melted and mixture is hot, stirring occasionally. Remove orange peel; discard.

Top individual servings of coffee mixture with dollop of whipped cream; sprinkle with cinnamon. Garnish as desired.
Makes about 6 servings

Variation: Add ¼ cup coffee-flavored liqueur to saucepan just before serving.

Beef & Zucchini Quiche

1 unbaked 9-inch pie shell
½ lb. lean ground beef
1 medium zucchini, shredded
3 green onions, sliced
¼ cup mushroom slices
1 tablespoon all-purpose flour
3 eggs, beaten
1 cup milk
¾ cup (3 ounces) shredded Swiss
  cheese
1½ teaspoons chopped fresh
  thyme or ½ teaspoon dried
  leaf thyme
½ teaspoon salt
  Dash of freshly ground black
  pepper
  Dash of ground red pepper

Preheat oven to 475°F.

Line pie shell with foil; fill with dried beans or rice. Bake 8 minutes. Remove from oven; carefully remove foil and beans. Return pie shell to oven. Continue baking 4 minutes; set aside. Reduce oven temperature to 375°F.

Brown ground beef in medium skillet. Drain. Add zucchini, onions and mushrooms; cook, stirring occasionally, until vegetables are tender. Stir in flour; cook 2 minutes, stirring constantly. Remove from heat.

Combine eggs, milk, cheese and seasonings in medium bowl. Stir into ground beef mixture; pour into crust.

Bake 35 minutes or until knife inserted near center comes out clean.
Makes 6 servings

Beef & Cabbage Puff

½ lb. lean ground beef
½ medium onion, chopped
3 cups finely shredded cabbage
1 teaspoon caraway seeds
1½ teaspoons chopped fresh
    thyme or ½ teaspoon dried
    leaf thyme
½ teaspoon salt
    Dash of freshly ground pepper
1 tablespoon all-purpose flour
¼ cup plain yogurt or sour cream
½ package (17½ oz.) frozen puff
    pastry (1 sheet), thawed

Preheat oven to 375°F.

Brown ground beef in medium skillet. Drain. Add onion; cook until tender. Stir in cabbage, caraway seeds and seasonings. Cook until cabbage is crisp-tender, stirring occasionally. Blend in flour. Remove from heat; stir in yogurt. Cool.

Place pastry on floured surface. Roll to 12 × 10-inch rectangle. Cut lengthwise in half to form two 12 × 5-inch rectangles. Spoon ground beef mixture down center of one rectangle to within 1 inch of outer edges. Fold remaining rectangle in half lengthwise; cut crosswise at 1-inch intervals from fold to about 1½ inches from opposite edge. Unfold rectangle. Moisten edges of rectangles. Place cut rectangle over filling, pressing edges of dough together to seal.

Bake 25 minutes or until puffed and golden brown.   *Makes 6 servings*

Cherry Streusel Coffeecake

1 cup cold water
1 (¼-ounce) package active
    dry yeast
½ cup sugar, divided
1 teaspoon salt
    About 4 cups all-purpose flour,
    divided
2 eggs, beaten
¼ cup butter or margarine,
    softened
1 teaspoon vanilla extract
1 (21-ounce) can cherry pie filling
    Crumb Topping (recipe follows)
¼ cup sliced almonds

Bring water to boil. Remove from heat; cool to lukewarm (110°). Pour into large bowl of electric mixer. Add yeast and 1 tablespoon sugar; mix until dissolved. Let stand 5 to 10 minutes or until foamy.

Add remaining sugar, the salt and 1 cup of the flour. Beat at medium speed 2 minutes. Add eggs, butter and vanilla; beat 1 minute. Stir in enough of the remaining 3 cups flour to make soft dough.

Knead dough on lightly floured surface 10 minutes or until dough is smooth and elastic. Cover with bowl. Let rest 10 minutes. On lightly floured board, roll dough to a 13 × 9-inch rectangle. Place in bottom of greased 13 × 9-inch baking pan. Press dough halfway up sides of pan to form rim. Spoon in pie filling; cover. Let rise in warm place until doubled in bulk, about 45 minutes.

Preheat oven to 350°F.

Prepare Crumb Topping. Sprinkle over pie filling; top with almonds.

Bake 30 minutes or until lightly browned. Cool.

Crumb Topping

½ cup all-purpose flour
½ cup sugar
¼ cup butter or margarine, chilled

Combine ingredients in small bowl. Cut in butter until mixture resembles coarse crumbs.
                    Makes about 12 servings

Note: Coffeecake can be made the day ahead.

Souper Nachos

¼ pound ground beef
2 envelopes LIPTON® Tomato
  Cup-a-Soup Instant Soup
½ cup water
1 teaspoon red wine vinegar
½ to 1 teaspoon chili powder
  Tortilla chips (about 30)
¼ cup chopped green onions
  (optional)
1 cup shredded Monterey Jack
  or Cheddar cheese
  (about 4 ounces)

In small microwave-safe bowl, microwave ground beef at HIGH (Full Power) 2 minutes or until no longer pink; drain. Stir in instant tomato soup mix, water, vinegar and chili powder. Microwave at HIGH 1½ minutes or until thickened, stirring once. Arrange ½ of the tortilla chips in one layer on microwave-safe plate, then top with ½ of the ground beef mixture, onions and cheese; repeat layer. Microwave at HIGH 1½ minutes or until cheese is melted.

Makes 4 snack-size or 1 main-dish serving

Conventional Directions: Preheat oven to 375°F. In small skillet, brown ground beef; drain. Stir in instant tomato soup mix, water, vinegar and chili powder. Cook, stirring frequently, 1 minute or until mixture thickens. Arrange as above on ovenproof plate or baking dish. Bake 10 minutes or until cheese is melted.

Traditional Party Mix

¼ cup (½ stick) margarine
1¼ teaspoons seasoned salt
4½ teaspoons worcestershire sauce
2⅔ cups CORN CHEX® Brand Cereal
2⅔ cups RICE CHEX® Brand Cereal
2⅔ cups WHEAT CHEX® Brand Cereal
1 cup salted mixed nuts
1 cup pretzel sticks

Preheat oven to 250°F. In open roasting pan melt margarine in oven. Remove. Stir in seasoned salt and worcestershire sauce. Gradually add cereals, nuts and pretzels, stirring until all pieces are evenly coated. Bake 1 hour, stirring every 15 minutes. Spread on absorbent paper to cool. Store in airtight container.   *Makes 9 cups*

Microwave directions : In a 4-quart bowl or 13 x 9 x 2-inch microwave-safe dish melt margarine on HIGH 1 minute. Stir in seasoned salt and worcestershire sauce. Gradually add cereals, nuts and pretzels, stirring until all pieces are evenly coated. Microwave on HIGH 5 to 6 minutes, stirring every 2 minutes. Spread on absorbent paper to cool. Store in airtight container.

Spinach Vegetable Dip

1 (16-ounce) container BORDEN®
  or MEADOW GOLD® Sour
  Cream
1 (10-ounce) package frozen
  chopped spinach, thawed
  and drained
1 (1.7-ounce) package MRS.
  GRASS® Homestyle Vegetable
  Recipe, Soup & Dip
2 tablespoons BORDEN® or
  MEADOW GOLD® Milk
  Melba rounds or crackers

In medium bowl, combine sour cream, spinach, dip mix and milk; mix well. Chill 3 hours to blend flavors. Stir before serving. Serve with Melba rounds. Refrigerate leftovers.

Makes about 4 cups

Clockwise from top left: Double Chocolate Football Cake (page 81), Souper Nachos and Glenn's Magic Chili (page 80).

Glenn's Magic Chili

This is best if made a day before serving.

2½ pounds lean, coarsely ground beef
2 tablespoons Chef Paul Prudhomme's MEAT MAGIC®
2 tablespoons chili powder
1 tablespoon dried oregano leaves
1½ teaspoons ground cumin
1 teaspoon salt
2 cups peeled, chopped tomatoes
2 cups very finely chopped onions
4 cups beef stock or water, in all
2 teaspoons minced garlic
1½ teaspoons Tabasco sauce
6 whole jalapeños with stems, about 4 ounces*
1 tablespoon corn flour or all-purpose flour
2 cups cooked pinto or red beans, optional

In 4-quart saucepan, combine meat, MEAT MAGIC®, chili powder, oregano, cumin and salt; stir well. Cover pan and cook over high heat 4 minutes. Stir well, re-cover pan and cook 1 minute. Stir in tomatoes and onions, re-cover pan and cook 10 minutes, stirring occasionally and scraping pan bottom well each time. Add 2 cups of the stock, the garlic and Tabasco sauce, stirring well. Stir in jalapeños. Bring to a boil, then reduce heat to low. Simmer 1 hour, stirring and scraping pan bottom occasionally. (Stir gently so that jalapeño skins don't break open.) Skim fat from top of chili mixture. Then in small bowl, stir together flour and 2 tablespoons of the liquid from chili mixture until well blended. Add flour mixture, 1 cup of the stock and the beans (if desired) to chili mixture, stirring well. Simmer 40 minutes, stirring frequently and gently and making sure mixture doesn't scorch (the flour makes it more likely to scorch). Add the remaining stock; cook and stir 20 minutes more. Serve hot in bowls, allowing about 1½ cups per serving. Garnish as desired.

Makes 4 servings without beans or 5 servings with beans

Note: If you make this a day ahead, remove jalapeños but reserve them to add back before reheating; be brave and give 'em a try—they really add flavor to chili!

*Fresh jalapeños are preferred; if you have to use pickled ones, rinse as much vinegar from them as possible. If jalapeño skins are broken, the seeds will escape into chili, giving the dish extra heat; if you like very hot chili, break one or more of the chilies open near the beginning of cooking time.

Copyright © 1986 by Paul Prudhomme

Country Cole Slaw

1 cup HELLMANN'S® or BEST FOODS® Real, Light or Cholesterol Free Reduced Calorie Mayonnaise
3 tablespoons lemon juice
2 tablespoons sugar
1 teaspoon salt
6 cups shredded cabbage
1 cup shredded carrots
½ chopped or thinly sliced green pepper

In medium bowl combine mayonnaise, lemon juice, sugar and salt. Stir in cabbage, carrots and green pepper. Cover; chill.

Makes about 10 servings

Double Chocolate Football Cake

Prep time: 30 minutes
Baking Time: 50 minutes

- **1 package (2-layer size) chocolate cake mix**
- **1 package (4-serving size) JELL-O® Instant Pudding and Pie Filling, Chocolate or Chocolate Fudge Flavor**
- **4 eggs**
- **1 cup water**
- **¼ cup vegetable oil**
  Easy Creamy Frosting (recipe follows)
  String licorice
  Candy corn
  BAKER'S® Semi-Sweet Real Chocolate Chips

COMBINE cake mix, pudding mix, eggs, water and oil in large bowl. Blend at low speed of electric mixer just to moisten, scraping sides of bowl often. Beat at medium speed 4 minutes. Pour into greased and floured 9-inch square pan. Bake at 325°F for 50 to 55 minutes or until cake tester inserted in center comes out clean and cake begins to pull away from sides of pan. (Do not underbake.) Cool in pan 15 minutes. Remove from pan; finish cooling on rack.

PLACE cake, right side up, on large cutting board. Cut as shown in Diagram 1, reserving outside corners for snacking or another use. Spread frosting over cake, mounding in center for rounded appearance. Decorate with licorice and candies to resemble football (Diagram 2). Chill until ready to serve.

Makes 12 servings

Easy Creamy Frosting

- **⅓ cup cold milk**
- **1 package (4-serving size) JELL-O® Instant Pudding, Chocolate or Chocolate Fudge Flavor**
- **1 teaspoon vanilla**
- **⅓ cup PARKAY® Margarine, softened**
- **3 cups confectioners sugar**

POUR milk into large bowl. Add pudding mix and vanilla; mix until smooth. Add margarine; blend well. Gradually blend in sugar, beating until smooth. (If mixture becomes too thick, add milk until frosting is of desired consistency.)

Makes about 2 cups

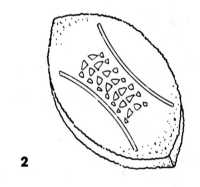

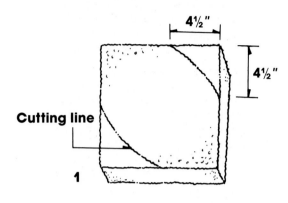

Mexican Shrimp Cocktail

½ cup WISH-BONE® Italian Dressing
½ cup chopped tomato
1 can (4 ounces) chopped green
  chilies, undrained
¼ cup chopped green onions
1½ teaspoons honey
¼ teaspoon hot pepper sauce
1 pound medium shrimp, cleaned
  and cooked
2 teaspoons finely chopped
  coriander (cilantro) or parsley

In medium bowl, combine Italian dressing, tomato, chilies, green onions, honey and hot pepper sauce. Stir in shrimp. Cover and marinate in refrigerator, stirring occasionally, at least 2 hours. Just before serving, stir in coriander.

Makes about 6 servings

Also terrific with WISH-BONE® Robusto Italian, Lite Italian, Blended Italian or Herbal Italian Dressing.

Calabacitas Con Elote

Cal-lah-bah-SEE-tas cone ay-LOW-tay —zucchini with corn—is a traditional Mexican side dish with serape-bright colors and garden-fresh flavors.

3 small zucchini, about 6 inches
  long, cut into ¼-inch slices
1 cup freshly cut corn kernels
  (cut from 2 to 3 ears) or 1 cup
  frozen corn, thawed
1 small red or green pepper, diced
1 small onion, chopped
1 garlic clove, minced
1 tablespoon butter or margarine
¼ teaspoon salt
⅓ cup PACE® picante sauce

Cook zucchini, corn, pepper, onion and garlic in butter in 10-inch skillet over medium-high heat, stirring constantly, about 2 minutes. Sprinkle with salt. Stir in picante sauce and continue cooking, stirring constantly, until most of liquid has evaporated and vegetables are crisp-tender, about 3 to 4 minutes.

Makes 6 servings

Guacamole-Chili Dip

1 medium avocado, peeled,
  seeded and cut up
1 tablespoon lemon juice
1 tablespoon finely chopped
  onion
1 small clove garlic, minced
¼ teaspoon salt
⅛ teaspoon hot pepper sauce
½ pound ground beef
½ cup chopped onion
1 can (11¾ ounces) CAMPBELL'S®
  Condensed Chili Beef Soup
1 cup shredded Cheddar cheese
  (4 ounces)
1 cup chopped lettuce
1 medium tomato, chopped

1. To prepare guacamole: In covered blender or food processor, combine first 6 ingredients; blend until smooth. Cover and set aside.

2. Crumble beef into 1½-quart microwave-safe casserole. Add ½ cup onion. Cover with lid; microwave on HIGH 3 minutes or until meat is no longer pink, stirring once to break up meat. Spoon off fat.

3. Stir in soup until well blended. Spread onto 10-inch microwave-safe platter. Sprinkle with cheese. Microwave, uncovered, on HIGH 2 minutes or until cheese is melted, rotating dish once during cooking.

4. Sprinkle lettuce and tomato over cheese; spoon guacamole in center. Serve with tortilla chips for dipping.

Makes 8 appetizer servings

Tip: Serve this hearty dip as a main dish. In step 3, divide soup mixture into four 10-ounce casseroles. Sprinkle with cheese. Microwave, uncovered, on HIGH 3 minutes or until cheese is nearly melted. Divide remaining ingredients among dishes.

Clockwise from top right: Caramel Flan (page 85), Calabacitas Con Elote and Beef and Bean Chimichangas (page 85).

Salsa Cruda

1 tablespoon vegetable oil
½ cup chopped onion
½ cup chopped celery
¾ cup V8® Vegetable Juice, divided
½ cup chopped green pepper
1 can (4 ounces) chopped chilies
1 tablespoon vinegar
¼ teaspoon hot pepper sauce

1. In small skillet over medium heat, in hot oil, cook onion and celery until tender-crisp, stirring often.

2. In covered blender or food processor, blend half of the cooked vegetable mixture and ¼ cup of the V8® juice until smooth.

3. In small bowl, stir together blended vegetable mixture, unblended vegetable mixture, remaining ½ cup V8® juice, green pepper, chilies, vinegar and hot pepper sauce. Cover; refrigerate until serving time, at least 2 hours. Use as a dip or as a filling for omelets. *Makes 2 cups*

White Sangria

½ to ¾ cup sugar
½ cup REALEMON® Lemon Juice from Concentrate, chilled
¼ cup REALIME® Lime Juice from Concentrate, chilled
1 (750-mL) bottle sauterne or other dry white wine, chilled
¼ cup orange-flavored liqueur
1 (32-ounce) bottle club soda, chilled
  Orange, plum or nectarine slices, green grapes or other fresh fruit
  Ice

In pitcher, combine sugar and juices; stir until sugar dissolves. Add sauterne and orange-flavored liqueur. Just before serving, add club soda, fruit and ice.
Makes about 2 quarts

Chili-Cheese Corn Muffins

MAZOLA® No Stick cooking spray
1 cup yellow corn meal
¾ cup flour
2 tablespoons sugar
1 tablespoon baking powder
¼ teaspoon salt
1 egg, lightly beaten
⅔ cup milk
⅓ cup HELLMANN'S® or BEST FOODS® Real, Light or Cholesterol Free Reduced Calorie Mayonnaise
1 can (7 ounces) corn or corn with green and red sweet peppers, drained
½ cup (2 ounces) shredded Cheddar cheese
3 to 6 tablespoons chopped green chilies, undrained

Spray 12 (2½-inch) muffin pan cups with cooking spray. In large bowl combine corn meal, flour, sugar, baking powder and salt. In small bowl combine egg, milk and mayonnaise; stir in corn, cheese and chilies until well mixed. Stir corn mixture into flour mixture just until moistened. Spoon into each prepared muffin pan cup. Bake in 400°F oven 20 to 25 minutes or until golden. Immediately remove from pan. Serve warm.
Makes 12 muffins

Enchiladas Acapulco

Preparation time: 25 minutes
Baking time: 28 minutes

1 lb. ground beef
1 8-oz. can tomato sauce
¾ cup chopped green pepper
1 8¾-oz. can kidney beans, drained
½ lb. VELVEETA® Mexican Pasteurized Process Cheese with Jalapeño Pepper, cubed
8 6-inch tortillas
  Oil
½ cup chopped tomato

In large skillet, brown meat; drain. Add sauce and ½ cup peppers; cook over medium heat 5 minutes, stirring occasionally. Add beans and ¼ lb. process cheese spread; continue cooking until process cheese spread is melted. Dip tortillas in hot oil to soften; drain. Fill each tortilla with ¼ cup meat mixture;

roll up. Place, seam side down, in 12×8-inch baking dish. Top with remaining meat mixture; cover. Bake at 350°, 20 minutes. Top with remaining process cheese spread; continue baking uncovered 5 to 8 minutes or until process cheese spread is melted. Top with tomatoes and remaining peppers.

4 servings

Variation: Substitute VELVEETA® Process Cheese Spread for Process Cheese Spread with Jalapeño Pepper.

Microwave: Omit oil. Crumble meat into 1½-quart microwave-safe bowl. Microwave on High 5 to 6 minutes, stirring after 3 minutes; drain. Stir in sauce and ½ cup peppers. Microwave on High 2 minutes. Stir in beans and ¼ lb. process cheese spread. Microwave on High 1 minute; stir until process cheese spread is melted. Wrap tortillas in dampened paper towels. Microwave on High 1 to 2 minutes or until softened. Assemble recipe as directed. Cover with plastic wrap; vent. Microwave on High 3 minutes or until thoroughly heated, turning dish after 1½ minutes. Top with remaining process cheese spread. Cover with plastic wrap; vent. Microwave on High 1 minute or until process cheese spread begins to melt. Top with tomatoes and remaining peppers.

Beef and Bean Chimichangas

    1 pound ground beef
    1 medium onion, chopped
    2 cloves garlic, minced
    1 can (14½ ounces) whole
        tomatoes, drained, cut up
    ⅓ cup salsa
    1½ teaspoons chili powder
    ¾ teaspoon ground coriander
    ½ teaspoon ground thyme
    ½ teaspoon salt
    ⅛ teaspoon cayenne
    ⅛ teaspoon ground cumin
    1 cup refried beans
        CRISCO® Oil for frying
    6 eight-inch flour tortillas
    ¾ cup shredded Monterey
        Jack cheese (optional)

Brown ground meat, onion and garlic in electric skillet at 365°F or in large heavy skillet over medium-high heat. Drain.

Stir in tomatoes, ⅓ cup salsa, chili powder, coriander, thyme, salt, cayenne and cumin. Cook over medium-low heat, stirring occasionally, 10 to 15 minutes, or until mixture is thickened. Remove from heat. Stir in refried beans.

Heat 2 or 3 inches CRISCO® Oil in deep-fryer or large saucepan to 365° F. Meanwhile, place ½ cup beef mixture in center of each tortilla. Fold opposite sides of tortilla to center over beef mixture. Fold ends toward center; secure with wooden pick.

Fry 1 or 2 chimichangas at a time, 1½ to 2 minutes, or until golden brown. Drain on paper towels. Sprinkle top of each chimichanga with 2 tablespoons Monterey Jack cheese (optional). Serve immediately with salsa, if desired.

6 servings

Caramel Flan

    ¾ cup sugar
    4 eggs
    1¾ cups water
    1 (14-ounce) can EAGLE® Brand
        Sweetened Condensed Milk
        (NOT evaporated milk)
    ½ teaspoon vanilla extract
    ⅛ teaspoon salt

Preheat oven to 350°F. In heavy skillet, over medium heat, cook sugar, stirring constantly until melted and caramel-colored. Pour into ungreased 9-inch round or square baking pan, tilting to coat bottom completely. In medium bowl, beat eggs; stir in water, sweetened condensed milk, vanilla and salt. Pour over caramelized sugar; set pan in larger pan (a broiler pan). Fill larger pan with 1 inch hot water. Bake 55 to 60 minutes or until knife inserted near center comes out clean. Cool. Chill thoroughly. Loosen side of flan with knife; invert onto serving plate with rim. Refrigerate leftovers. ***Makes 10 to 12 servings***

Fresh Corn on the Grill

**6 ears corn, with silk and husks intact
Butter or margarine
Salt and pepper**

Turn back corn husks; do not remove. Remove silks with stiff brush; rinse corn. Lay husks back into position. Roast ears, on covered grill, over medium-hot **KINGSFORD® Briquets** about 25 minutes or until tender, turning corn often. Remove husks and serve with butter, salt and pepper, as desired.

Makes 6 servings

Great American Potato Salad

*Preparation time:
30 minutes plus chilling*

**1 cup MIRACLE WHIP® Salad Dressing
1 teaspoon KRAFT® Pure Prepared Mustard
½ teaspoon celery seed
½ teaspoon salt
⅛ teaspoon pepper
4 cups cubed cooked potatoes
2 hard-cooked eggs, chopped
½ cup chopped onion
½ cup celery slices
½ cup chopped sweet pickle**

Combine salad dressing, mustard, celery seed, salt and pepper; mix well. Add remaining ingredients; mix lightly. Cover; chill. Garnish with celery leaves, if desired.

Makes 6 servings

Variations: Omit celery and pickle. Add 1½ cups chopped ham and ½ cup chopped green pepper.

Omit celery seed, celery and pickles. Add 1 cup chopped cucumber and ½ teaspoon dill weed.

Omit mustard, celery seed and pickles. Add 3 tablespoons SAUCEWORKS® Horseradish Sauce and 1½ cups cubed roast beef.

Fresh Fruit Kabobs

**½ cup butter or margarine, softened
⅓ cup honey
1 large fresh pineapple, cored, peeled and cut into 1-inch cubes
3 fresh apricots, peaches or nectarines, cut into pieces
1 jar (4 ounces) maraschino cherries, drained**

Combine butter and honey. Beginning and ending with pineapple, thread fruit pieces alternately on skewers. Brush kabobs with butter-honey mixture. Grill kabobs over medium-hot **MATCH LIGHT® Charcoal Briquets** 3 to 5 minutes or until fruit is heated through. Turn once or twice and brush with butter-honey mixture. Serve with pound cake, ice cream or whipped topping, if desired.

Melon Wedges

**1 cantaloupe or honeydew melon
1 package (4-serving size) JELL-O® Brand Apricot or Orange Flavor Sugar Free Gelatin
1 cup boiling water
¾ cup cold water
1 banana, sliced, ½ cup sliced strawberries or 1 can (8¼ ounces) crushed pineapple in juice, well drained**

Cut melon in half lengthwise; scoop out seeds and drain well. Dissolve gelatin in boiling water. Add cold water. Chill until slightly thickened. Stir in fruit. Pour into melon halves. Chill until firm, about 3 hours. Cut in wedges. Serve with additional fresh fruit, cottage cheese and crisp greens, if desired.

Makes 6 servings

Note: Chill any excess fruited gelatin in dessert dish.

Clockwise from top: Ranch Burgers (page 88), Fresh Corn on the Grill, Chili Dogs (page 88) and Great American Potato Salad.

Chili Dogs

Top this New York original with assorted condiments: pickles, relishes, sauerkraut, peppers, onions, mustard, ketchup, or, as for this Coney Island-style frank, chili.

½ pound ground beef
2 teaspoons chili powder
⅛ teaspoon ground cumin
1 can (16 ounces) CAMPBELL'S® Pork & Beans in Tomato Sauce
2 tablespoons chopped and seeded VLASIC® Mild or Hot Cherry Peppers
8 frankfurters
8 frankfurter buns, split and toasted
½ cup finely chopped onion

1. To make chili: In 2-quart saucepan over medium heat, cook beef, chili powder and cumin until no pink remains in meat, stirring to separate meat. Spoon off fat. Stir in beans, pressing with spoon to mash slightly. Stir in peppers; heat to boiling. Reduce heat to low; simmer, uncovered, 10 minutes, stirring occasionally.

2. On grill rack, arrange frankfurters directly above medium-hot coals. Grill, uncovered, 5 to 8 minutes or until heated through, turning often. Place frankfurters in buns. Spoon about ¼ cup chili and 1 tablespoon onion over each.

Makes 8 servings

Lemony Light Cooler

3 cups white grape juice or white wine
½ cup REALEMON® Lemon Juice from Concentrate
½ cup sugar
1 (32-ounce) bottle club soda, chilled
Green grapes, strawberries and orange slices
Ice

In pitcher, combine grape juice, REALEMON® brand and sugar; stir until sugar dissolves. Just before serving, add club soda and fruit. Serve over ice.

Makes about 7 cups

Ranch Burgers

1¼ pounds lean ground beef
¾ cup prepared HIDDEN VALLEY RANCH® Original Ranch® salad dressing
¾ cup dry bread crumbs
¼ cup minced onions
1 teaspoon salt
¼ teaspoon black pepper
Sesame seed buns
Lettuce, tomato slices and red onion slices (optional)
Additional Original Ranch® salad dressing

In large bowl, combine beef, salad dressing, bread crumbs, onions, salt and pepper. Shape into 6 patties. Grill over medium-hot coals 4 to 5 minutes for medium doneness. Place on sesame seed buns with lettuce, tomato and red onion slices, if desired. Serve with a generous amount of additional salad dressing.

Serves 6

Over-the-Coals Spiced Popcorn

½ cup popcorn or 8 cups popped popcorn
2 tablespoons butter or margarine
½ teaspoon Worcestershire sauce
½ teaspoon chili powder
½ teaspoon lemon pepper
¼ teaspoon garlic powder
¼ teaspoon onion powder
⅛ teaspoon salt

If desired, pop ½ cup popcorn over briquets in long-handled fireplace corn popper. Hold directly over, but not touching, hot KINGSFORD® Briquets; shake vigorously until corn is popped, about 3 to 4 minutes

In saucepan, combine remaining ingredients. Set on edge of grill to melt butter. Toss butter mixture with popped popcorn.

Makes about 8 cups

Drizzle-Topped Brownies

1¼ cups all-purpose biscuit baking
    mix
1 cup sugar
½ cup HERSHEY'S® Cocoa
½ cup butter or margarine, melted
2 eggs
1 teaspoon vanilla extract
1 cup HERSHEY'S® Semi-Sweet
    Chocolate Chips or
    MINI CHIPS®
    Quick Vanilla Glaze (recipe
    follows)

Heat oven to 350°F. Grease 8- or 9-inch square baking pan. In medium bowl combine baking mix, sugar and cocoa; mix with spoon or fork until thoroughly blended. Add butter, eggs and vanilla, mixing well. Stir in chocolate chips. Spread into prepared pan. Bake 25 to 30 minutes or until wooden pick inserted in center comes out clean. Cool completely. Drizzle Quick Vanilla Glaze over cooled brownies. Cut into bars.   *About 20 brownies*

Quick Vanilla Glaze:

In small bowl, combine ½ cup confectioners' sugar, 1 tablespoon water and ¼ teaspoon vanilla extract; blend well.

Deep Dish Peach Cobbler

1 package DUNCAN HINES® Spice
    Cake Mix
1 cup quick-cooking oats (not
    instant or old-fashioned)
1 cup chopped walnuts
¾ cup butter or margarine, melted
6 cups peeled and sliced
    peaches (about 6 large)
½ cup water
3 tablespoons brown sugar
2 tablespoons cornstarch
1 tablespoon plus 1 teaspoon
    lemon juice
    Whipped topping, for garnish
    Nutmeg, for garnish

1. Preheat oven to 350°F. Grease and flour 13 x 9 x 2-inch pan.

2. Combine cake mix, oats, nuts and butter in large bowl. Stir until well blended. Press 2½ cups mixture in bottom of pan. Set aside remaining mixture.

3. Combine peaches, water and brown sugar in large saucepan. Simmer on low heat 5 minutes, stirring occasionally. Combine cornstarch and lemon juice in cup. Gradually add to peaches. Stir until thickened. Pour over crust. Sprinkle reserved crumbs evenly over peaches. Bake at 350°F for 25 to 30 minutes or until topping is lightly browned. Serve with whipped topping sprinkled with nutmeg, if desired.   *10 to 12 servings*

Tip: Also great served with ice cream.

Chocolate Stripe Cake

1 package (18.25 ounces) white
    cake mix
1 envelope unflavored gelatin
¼ cup cold water
¼ cup boiling water
1 cup HERSHEY'S® Syrup
    Whipped topping
    HERSHEY'S® Syrup (optional
    garnish)

Heat oven to 350°F. Grease and flour 13 x 9 x 2-inch baking pan. Prepare cake batter and bake according to package directions. Cool 15 minutes. Do not remove cake from pan. With fork carefully pierce cake to bottom of pan, making rows about 1 inch apart covering length and width of cake. In small bowl sprinkle gelatin over cold water; let stand 1 minute to soften. Add boiling water; stir until gelatin is completely dissolved and mixture is clear. Stir in 1 cup syrup. Pour chocolate mixture evenly over cooled cake, making sure entire top is covered and mixture has flowed into holes. Cover; chill about 5 hours or until set. Serve with whipped topping; garnish with syrup, if desired. Refrigerate leftovers.   *12 to 15 servings*

Glazed Popcorn

8 cups popped popcorn
¼ cup butter or margarine
3 tablespoons light corn syrup
½ cup packed light brown sugar
  or granulated sugar
1 package (4-serving size) JELL-O®
  Brand Gelatin, any flavor

Place popcorn in large bowl. Heat butter and syrup in small saucepan over low heat. Stir in brown sugar and gelatin; bring to a boil over medium heat. Reduce heat to low and gently simmer for 5 minutes. Pour syrup immediately over popcorn, tossing to coat well. Spread popcorn into aluminum-foil-lined 15 × 10 × 1-inch pan, using two forks to spread evenly. Bake in preheated 300°F oven for 10 minutes. Cool. Remove from pan and break into small pieces. *Makes 2 quarts*

Fast 'n Fun Pasta Pizza

Ready to bake in just 15 easy minutes.

3 cups fusilli or elbow macaroni,
  cooked in unsalted water and
  drained
1 pound ground beef
1 jar (15½ ounces) spaghetti
  sauce
2 eggs, slightly beaten
1 can (2.8 ounces) DURKEE® French
  Fried Onions
⅓ cup (about 1½ ounces) grated
  Parmesan cheese
  Assorted toppings: chopped
  green pepper, sliced
  mushrooms, DURKEE® olives
1 cup (4 ounces) shredded
  Mozzarella cheese

Preheat oven to 375°F. In medium skillet, brown ground beef; drain. Stir in spaghetti sauce; reduce heat and simmer, uncovered, 5 minutes.

In medium bowl, combine hot pasta, eggs, ½ can French Fried Onions and the Parmesan cheese. Spread pasta mixture over greased 12-inch pizza pan. Top with ground beef mixture and desired toppings. Bake, covered, at 375° for 25 minutes or until heated through. Top with mozzarella cheese and remaining onions; bake, uncovered, 3 minutes or until onions are golden brown. Cut into wedges to serve.
Makes 4 to 6 servings

Carrot Salad

Preparation time: 15 minutes

2 cups shredded carrots
2 cups chopped apples
½ cup MIRACLE WHIP® Salad
  Dressing
½ cup raisins
½ cup chopped pecans

Combine ingredients; mix lightly.
Makes 6 servings

Variation: Substitute MIRACLE WHIP® Light Reduced Calorie Salad Dressing for Regular Salad Dressing

Food processor tip: To shred carrots, use shredding disk of food processor.

Creamy Hot Chocolate

1 can (14 ounces) EAGLE® Brand
  Sweetened Condensed Milk
  (NOT evaporated milk)
½ cup unsweetened cocoa
1½ teaspoons vanilla extract
⅛ teaspoon salt
6½ cups hot water
  Whipped cream, optional

In large saucepan, combine sweetened condensed milk, cocoa, vanilla and salt. Over medium heat, slowly stir in water; heat through, stirring occasionally. Garnish with whipped cream if desired.
Makes about 2 quarts

Clockwise from top left: Jack-o'-Lantern Pie (page 92), Hot Mulled Cider (page 92), Glazed Popcorn and Fast 'n Fun Pasta Pizza.

Acknowledgments

*The Publishers would like to thank the companies and organizations
listed below for the use of their recipes in this book.*

Bel Paese Sales Company
Best Foods, a Division of CPC International Inc.
Borden, Inc.
Campbell Soup Company
Checkerboard Kitchens, Ralston Purina Company
Chef Paul Prudhomme's Magic Seasoning Blends™
The Creamette Company
Domino® Sugars
Durkee-French Foods, a Division of Reckitt & Coleman Inc.
Filippo Berio
Hershey Foods Corporation
The HVR Company
Kellogg Company
Kikkoman International Inc.
The Kingsford Products Company
Kraft General Foods, Inc.
Lawry's Foods, Inc.
McIlhenny Company
National Live Stock & Meat Board
Pace Foods, Inc.
The Procter & Gamble Company, Inc.
Rice Council
Thomas J. Lipton, Inc.

INDEX

continued

PUBLISHERS CLEARING HOUSE has a wide variety of unbeatable magazine values available by subscription. Among the titles are TV GUIDE, U.S. NEWS, LADIES HOME JOURNAL, COOKING LIGHT and many more. To order please write to:

PUBLISHERS CLEARING HOUSE
101 WINNERS CIRCLE • PORT WASHINGTON, NEW YORK 11050